LIVE YOUR *FAITH*
OUT LOUD

Presented by

DOROTHY P. WILSON

Shirley "Cuz" Jackson
Kingdom Build!
By Telling your Story! !
Every Story Matters!

For more information or to request interviews:
http://www.livingfaithoutloud.com/faithinspiration
dwilson@dwilsonandassociates.com

ISBN: 978-1-7366846-0-3
First Printing, April 2021

DEDICATION

To Ella Chaney Patrick
March 23, 1927 - March 13, 2019

Momma, thank you for believing I could do anything and cheering the loudest for me. Your beautiful spirit will always live on through me and the countless others whose lives you touched with your soft smile and humble spirit.

"You never know what a person's going through," you'd always say. You inspired me to appreciate each person, individually, right where they are standing, no matter their issues, no matter their past or present.

CONTENTS

FOREWORD

From Pastor Jordan Ducote
Northwood Church

A significant moment in every believer's life is when they realize that they aren't just serving or worshiping God in the four walls of their local church, but are doing so in their everyday life, whether it's on the job, at school, or just at home. The revelation of being a living sacrifice unto God is a perspective shift that affects everything we do. As a pastor, it's one of the things you hope to see in the life of the members of your church. It's encouraging to see a book devoted to inspiring others to live their faith out loud.

"Live Your Faith Out Loud" encourages all of us to be a person that doesn't just live out their faith on Sunday, but on Monday through Saturday, too. Each of us has walked through different situations and have different experiences and gifts that God wants to use to draw people to Himself, but we have to be willing to surrender who we are to what He wants us to be.

As you read this book, you'll see stories of heartache, inspiration and creativity that will challenge you to live your faith in a more meaningful way. I'm excited to see how God uses this project to build His kingdom.

Pastor Jordan Ducote
and his wife, Nadine

Ducote is senior pastor at Northwood Church, whose mission is to build Christ-centered communities that help people to know God, grow in Christ, and go in the power of the Holy Spirit until Jesus returns. Northwood Church has campuses in Gulfport, Wiggins, Long Beach and Ocean Springs, Miss.

FAITHINSPIRATION PROJECT
FOUNDING SUPPORTERS

Thank you for believing in this dream

Mercedes Carranza
Robin Harris
Bonnie Collins
Richard Mitchell
Nell Cowart
Karol Brandt
Ashley Robertson
Robert Middleton
Eric White
Rose Coleman
Quandara Grant
Willie Brown
Barbara White Smalls
Smathe Toles
Koren Pope
Davina Coleman
Phylecia Rivers
Kenneth White
Janetha White
Thomas Bellamy Jr.
Nakeisha Thompson
Kasaundra Frye
Sarah Laguerre
De'Erica Gallion
Overseer Eric Ward I
Vera Goodloe
Eric Ward II
William Hardy
Kelly Spinner
Katherine "Kathy" Watts

Misty Cowart
Sonja Bunch
Shanna Pegues
Terry Fountain
Edwina Sumrall
Dr. Margaret Dawson
Anita Baham
Patrick Payton
Tywana Blackston
William Scott
LaToya Johnson
Shirley Jackson
Victoria Sharpe
Jennifer Anderson
First Lady Catherine Henderson
Keith Harris
Angie Johnston
Shalon Barnett
Dr. Tylisha Johnson
Amos Troublefield
Joyce M. Miles
Andrea McKinney
Rotesa Baker
Aretha Sparks
Sandra Blue-Harris
Yolanda Penny
Shaquilla Hill
B.R. Jackson
Terrie Fleming
Evangelist C.J. Johnson

FAITHINSPIRATION PROJECT
FOUNDING SUPPORTERS

Dianne and Larry Pope

Andria Warren

Jessie Clark

Gloria Ross

Clarence Webb

Pennie and Andy Williams

Christina Turner

Flora Addison

Yasuko Webb

James Darrell Wilson

Darlene Bruce

Michelle Baily

Sacoria Lucas

Danny Price

Jerrika Jackson

Dawn Wilson

Hermolee Thomas Barnes

Carleeka Basnight-Menendez

Tangelia Smith

Vanessa D. Brown

Cynthia Wolfinger

Gertrude Smith

Angelyn Treutel Zeringue

Jawea Howard

Tricia Allen

Sharon Brown

Shantel Fraizer

Jeanette Sears

Faith Glas-Miller

Delores Allen

Doris Shed

Kimberly Thornton

Donna Thompson

Daisy Wiliamson

Denise Millan

Racquel Rochelle

Candace Stevens

Lisa Jarvis

Karen Cockerham

Renee Norman

Adam Brady

Marina Crisler

Deborah Holmes Washington

Valencia Fairley

Andrea Riley

Marcia Miller

Jan Saunders

Latoya Griggs

Rebecca Byrd

Susan Parish

Vanetta Arnold

Dorian Hunter

Erika Henry

Evelyn Dunn

Trey Dunn

Paulla Shaw

Bob and Shana Morant

Sue Cole

Alice Bell

Annette Hardin

Mari Arnold

Cheryl Bradley Alston

Amy Pinkerman

Michelle Henry

FAITHINSPIRATION PROJECT
FOUNDING SUPPORTERS

Shannon Meadows
Veronica Carter
Peggy Jones
Viola Wellington
Tori May
Mark Watkins
Jacquelyn and Glenn Wright
Shelia Humphrey Morris
Jennifer Smith
Deborah Woods
Robin Banks
Cheryl King
Mary Hubbard
Beverly Gibson
Judy Lucas
Mary Cokley
Brenda Dollar
Tori King
Daisy King
Melanie Miller
Eunice Mann
Angela Moore
Avis and Rockie Pitts
Billie Boyd-Cox
Judy Lucas
Dr. Toni Alvarado
Racquel Gardener
Andrea Riley
Porsha Bush
Ben and Samantha Bergeron
Davy and Tracy McCarty
Vera Aubert
Justin and Kristen Fayard

Michael and Betty Shepard
Ron and Sandra Williams
Paul Wangerin and Stacey Trest
Tim and Karla Brady
Nichole and Jeannie Rankin
Frances Neathery
Rachel and Robert Starkey
Dave and Marianne Thomas
Michael and Lana Wangerin
Kristina Broussard
Cynthia Broussard
Russell Fishkind
Nathan Ladner
Benita Patterson
Eula Davis
Mark Fleming
Latoshia Manigo
Rodney Hamilton
Carolyn Green
Beverly Ferguson
Tammy Oglesby
Deacon Pierce Thompkins
Cynthia Walker
Lucille Batts
Adara Houston
Prophetess Diane Gilmore
Reesa Crisson
Alexis Houston
Phillip Jones
NellyJean Young
Donna Freeman
Veronica Carter
Joyce Chilton

Can't Never Will

From Dorothy P. Wilson
FaithInspiration Project Visionary

One Sunday morning at church, a visiting bishop from South Africa, short in stature but with a booming voice, exclaimed, "You can do MORE!" I thought, "Boy, he's passionate. I'd say I'm pretty busy right now serving as a small group leader and helping to lead in the children's ministry. Whew, I am worn out!" Bishop Edom Hopson obviously didn't hear my thoughts because he kept on: "You can do MORE!"

As my spirit opened up to really hear and receive the bishop's message, I received his words a little differently. I understood that for whom much is given, much is required, and God has worked overtime to fix the wounded, angry girl I once was. Not only had He delivered me from unforgiveness, fear, rejection, pride (hopefully I'm at the point where I'm beginning to finish up that particular training module!) and insecurity, He also healed me from fibromyalgia. And He continues to tackle me with blessings that flow from His love every day. Yes, I could do MORE.

Inspired, I began to reach further outside the walls of the church to impact my community, to empower thousands of women, even when I felt I didn't have the time. And now I understand: The more I pour myself out, the more God pours into me. Hallelujah!

He spoke to me one morning while I was driving to work and showed me that He was waiting to pour more into me, and that I was the one who had to make room for it!

That set me on a path to do bigger and greater things to further God's Kingdom and to bless His people. I am blessed to be a blessing!

In 2020, I began to get a fuzzy vision of publishing a book about how others could live their faith louder. I wasn't sure of the details, so I just let that thing sit there. God came back and started adding to the vision. I knew this wouldn't just be another book I produced. I have received the recognition of being the editor/project manager of a New York Times best-seller and an Amazon best-seller, and people keep asking me about a little pocket-sized

---

"What does it profit, my brethren, if someone says he has faith but does not have works? Can faith save him?"
— JAMES 2:14

book, "Little Book of Weapons: How To Defeat Your Giants", I published back in 2011.

And then one morning as I was hurriedly getting dressed for work, I heard God say, "It's time to begin." I knew He meant it was time for me to move forward with the FaithInspiration Project, which included a book with the title He gave me: "Live Your Faith Out Loud." I believe He trusted that I would be willing to go big on this, but inside I was really scared. What if it flops? What if it doesn't get picked up by churches? What if I can't get enough authors to partner with me?

I remembered what my friend Kathy Rogers once said to me: Think of that "what if" in a positive way. So, I shifted my thinking. What if this project was not only a book but also a series of videos and blog posts? And a small group discussion guide. Wow. What if this project really took off and touched people all over the world?

And I also chuckled as I recalled something I heard my school-teacher son say to his students: "Can't never will."

Enough said. It was go time.

God already has made provision for this project to be successful. I pray that you will be touched by the stories — lives — shared within this book, and that you will be compelled to Live Your Faith Out Loud.

It's go time for you, too. You can do more!

Project visionary Dorothy P. Wilson, of Gulfport, Miss. is an award-winning publisher and editor. She has worked in media for 30-plus years and currently publishes Gulf Coast Woman and Gulf Coast Weddings magazines; co-hosts the "I See You" show; is managing partner of CWR Digital Gulf Coast; is co-founder of Success Women's Conference, which reaches over 17,000 people at its annual summit; and is president and owner of DWilson & Associates, a publishing and marketing services firm. She has been named an SBA Women Business Champion, one of the Top Most Influential African-Americans in the State of Mississippi; and a Top 10 Woman Business Owner by the National Association of Women Business Owners. She and her husband, James, have two sons, James Evan and James Patrick.

2

CHAPTER 1

Saved to Save Others

By Elder Nicole S. Mason, Esquire

My life changed forever on June 7, 1992. I found myself in a hail of gunfire, unsure of whether I was going to live or die. You see, at that time in my life, I was living in two worlds. This is a reality for many African-Americans who grow up in urban centers. Before you turn the page, let me explain what I mean. On the one hand, I was an excellent student. In fact, I had graduated from Howard University 29 days before this life-altering event happened in my life. On the other hand, I was faced with a decision every day about whether to maintain friendships with others in my neighborhood who had not chosen the same path as I. In other words, I was mingling with the "wrong crowd."

Now, it is important to note that this is not an easy decision to make. Yet, the old adage is true: "You are guilty by association." Well, my beloved grandmother warned me over and over again, "Nicky, you are not like the people you are hanging around." My response to her was, "Aw, Grandma, you don't know what you're talking about. These people are my friends." Of course, you can see where this story is heading.

On that fateful night, I was doing what I did almost every weekend — going to a party. But before heading to the party, I did what I did almost every day. I drove through the neighborhood to see if I could "hook up" with him. No, he wasn't my boyfriend. It was a "hook up." I don't need to give you any additional details, so you don't have to put the book down trying to figure out what kind of book is this exactly. I can hear you now saying to yourself, "I thought this was a book about living your faith out loud." Yep, it is absolutely about me living my faith out loud. But it is important for you to understand why I am so passionate about my faith.

As we sat in my car, two men crept up on the passenger side of the car and began firing into the car. The only way that I have been able to describe what happened next is to say that God stepped out of Heaven, pulled me out of the car and pushed me down the street. It was as if I blacked out, because I don't have any recollection of opening the car door. However, I do remember that when there was some distance between the threat and safety, I became fully aware.

As I ran, I could still hear gunshots behind me. I thought I had been shot. So, my body began to respond to my thoughts. I didn't have the strength to run any longer. My breath was shallow, and my legs were like jelly. The moment that I thought about getting on my hands and knees to crawl, I looked up, and there were a man and woman standing on their porch. They didn't ask me any questions. They just hurriedly told me to come in and lie down on the floor. I told them that the men had shot the guy sitting in the car with me. The man called 911. I also asked to call my sister. I was attempting to run to her house. God strategically placed the man and woman on the porch to wait for me to help me.

My friend was murdered, and I ended up being a witness in the case. As I waited for the murder trial of the shooter to begin, I was invited to a church. I knew when I walked into the church that I belonged there. On September 26, 1993, I gave my heart to the Lord. Due to space constraints, I can't share all of the ways that God met me, but I will share this with you. I didn't get the names of the people who helped me that night, but I did have a detailed description of them. My sister picked me up from the house, and she watched me walk out of the house. My mom went back to the house approximately two weeks later. She merely wanted to thank the man and woman who had helped me that night, but she didn't have their names. After my mom gave the lady who answered the door the detailed descriptions that I had given her of the man and woman, she told my mom that no one by those descriptions had ever lived there. I know. I know. Take a deep breath. Yep, God had dispatched angels to save me that night.

I can confidently say that my life is not my own. I can also unequivocally say that God saved me that night for a purpose. You, too, have purpose assigned to your life. Since that happened to me, I have come to know and embrace that God has a plan for us all. I can say emphatically that I have never looked back. I left the partying and all the people who were not going in the same direction. Of course, I came to the painstaking realization that my grandmother was right, and she sure knew what she was talking about. I wasn't like the people I was hanging out with. I had a call on my life to make an impact and to make a difference. So, that's exactly what I've been doing.

I knew at 9 years old that I wanted to be a lawyer. After applying to law school nine times and being rejected nine times, I was finally accepted into law school. Yep, you read that correctly. I was rejected nine times. But, God knew that I was not mentally prepared to go into the rigorous study of law school after enduring the murder of my friend and what was supposed to be a murder trial but turned into a plea deal offered to the shooter. I was eventually accepted to law school on the tenth attempt. I went on the pass the bar exam and started my own law practice. Additionally, I started a ministry to encourage and empower other women. I started a newsletter with an initial distribution of approximately 125 women in my local church. The newsletter mailing list quickly grew to more than 2,500 women all across the country. Many of the women on my mailing list were women serving time in prison. People were sending the newsletter to their loved ones in prison, and the women were writing me letting me know how much my words were a blessing to them.

I also have been a public servant working for the federal government. I currently serve as the first African-American female on my organization's senior management team. I have impacted many people over the years with my faith because of the light that shines brightly from within. I have learned that I don't have to call the name of the Lord in the marketplace as much as I have to live a life that would cause others to see the light, to live a life that causes others to become curious about the difference they see in how I relate to others and how I model Godly principles. Wherever I have worked, my office has been a safe haven for people to share their lives with me. I have offered advice, salvation, comfort, feedback, a shoulder to lean on to face some of life's most difficult challenges. Most importantly, I have offered love.

As I close this chapter, the one thing that I am sure of and confident in is the fact that I was saved to save others. To me, the church is where I go to get filled up and then go out into the world to spread the love of God in the marketplace. Matthew 9:12 says, "It is not the healthy who need a doctor, but the sick." As a disciple, I have a duty to take the medicine of the Word to those that need it the most. And those people are not within the four walls of the church. But above all, we all should embody the Gospel and have enough wisdom about how to appropriately spread the Gospel. This speaks to one's own dedication, commitment, and discipline in maintaining her own relationship with God and keeping God a top priority. One can never give what one doesn't have! People aren't impressed with titles and how many scriptures we know. Titles don't save. Titles don't deliver. Titles don't heal. Jesus does, and He uses people who know who they are, who He is, and people who know how to effectively share Him with those in the marketplace. People, are, however impacted by the way we treat them and how we humanize this Jesus whom we love so much!

Nicole Mason is a leader in both the ministry and the marketplace. She is intentional on living by example. She started in ministry 19 years ago with a newsletter and approximately 125 women in her home church. Her audience quickly swelled to more than 2,500 women all over the country, including women who were incarcerated.

CHAPTER 2

On the Other Side of Loss

By Brian Pearse

November 14, 2006, is a day that I wish I could forget but never will. A day I wish I could erase and eliminate from the calendar. But the universe simply does not work that way. It was a day that made me think I did not know who or what I was. I had been plunged into an abyss of despair, depression, despondency, and defeat.

This was a day like any other day of the year. I had awakened, sent the kids off to school, and gone to work. It was a day that had slightly special meaning, because my son, Jameel, would finally take his test for his permit to drive. He was in no rush to get his license, perhaps because he enjoyed the benefits of being in a household with three licensed drivers who were his own personal Uber drivers. I, too, was in no rush for him to obtain his permit to drive, because my car insurance payment would dramatically increase. His presence on my policy would double the rate because he was a male under the age of 25. When my daughter, Kiara, was added to the policy, it merited only a slight increase, but the boy would double the rate. The budget would have to be adjusted to handle the increase.

I moved throughout the day, and I do not remember much of the morning. I knew that evening I had to go to a fundraiser dinner, and I wasn't extremely excited about it. I'm just not the fundraising type of guy. I had stopped by my friend Allen's office, perhaps to solicit a donation, when my wife, Yvette, called and said that the police had called her and said Kiara had been in an accident. Then she said to meet her at the hospital.

Allen said he would go with me; he was godfather to Jameel. My mind, of course, began to race, but this was not Kiara's first fender bender, so I was not overwhelmed with grave thoughts. I think I drove myself; honestly, I do not remember.

Upon arriving at the hospital, I remember seeing a helicopter on the landing pad, and the blades were still rotating clockwise, circulating slowly. Time was moving slowly, and for some reason I entered the hospital via the entrance nearest to the helicopter pad. Why? I do not know… I wanted quick access, and the door was open. When I entered, I looked left over my shoulder and saw Kiara lying on a gurney. Time froze; I froze. Then I was quickly escorted out of this area to the front where my wife was. The next thing I remember is being asked what type of medical insurance I had. At the same time, I had questions. Where was my son, and what was the status of my children? No answers were coming forward, only the constant request for insurance information. Truly, that was the last thing I was concerned about. I knew I had insurance; I was a veteran. My children had medical insurance. I just wanted to know if they were okay. No information was forthcoming.

After the issue of insurance was settled, we were taken to a room. We only wanted information, and, still, none was coming forth. Time seemed to creep. Slowly, the room began to fill with people, a few doctors and others. I quickly learned one individual was a social worker. This is when they began to tell us the status of Kiara and Jameel, and the information was devastating. My life was forever changed. We were told Kiara was dead. Jameel was being taken to surgery to repair the injuries he sustained. To say my world was rocked is an understatement. I do not remember if we were asked or just told we could go see Kiara, but we went. When we were escorted down the corridor I had just traveled, it reminded me of the Green Mile movie as they traveled to the death chamber. I was traveling to meet death also. As I entered the room, Kiara was lying on the gurney, lifeless. All I could do was fall to my knees and cry out in pain. Kiara, my firstborn; Kiara my high school senior; Kiara, my beautiful daughter, lay on a gurney dead. As I write this, I'm crying; these memories are painful. Embracing this pain is hard! But it is necessary for my healing. Mind you, it has been 14 years, and these thoughts break me still.

We were again escorted back down the corridor to the room of tissue boxes and people. I met with the coroner, who looked like walking death himself, and then I was told briefly of Jameel's status. He was in surgery. Somehow I had to shut off the emotions and pain of losing Kiara and focus on Jameel, hoping for him to pull through surgery and survive the crash. The hospital was filled with friends of the kids; my phone was blowing up. I was being overwhelmed with love and support. It was a lot to comprehend, a lot to process. I truly shut down thoughts of Kiara and did not process her death then. I became a prayer warrior for Jameel. Sometimes I think I may have failed that night with prayer. I'm thankful for the saints of God, who will be intercessors and pray for you, those who will pick up your cross and help you with your burden.

Hours passed as Yvette and I awaited some good news about Jameel's status. Soon a small entourage of doctors — with no social worker — came to brief us on his status. The news was not good. There was no brain activity, and he sustained multiple internal injuries. There was mention of transferring him to a different hospital, but they gave little hope of change in his status. Basically, the machines and chemicals in his body were keeping him alive. We were told when the chemicals wore down, he would die. A nursed asked if we wanted to hold his hand as he died. I think I declined, to the nurse's surprise. Yvette said he is already gone. We waited in the room only to have another meeting with the coroner. The social worker, a church member, was there with us during this time. My friend Allen was there, and my pastor, who had been out of town, made it back and was with us. Seven hours had passed since the news of Kiara, and now both of my children were gone. We were driven home and left alone in our home. My, what a day November 14, 2006, had become. Who and what was to become of me, I surely did not know. I just wanted to wake up from this horrendous nightmare I was living.

How does one live after such tragedy and misfortune, losing two beautiful children on the same day? I felt like life was over. One really does not want to go on after losing so much. Kiara and Jameel were our only children. Kiara was a senior, so we would not witness her graduation day. No weddings to plan. No grandchildren to spoil. No one to pass family heirlooms on to. Nothing but a premature empty nest, and us filled with questions of "what ifs" and memories.

How does a parent survive, continue to even want to live, after such devastating news? At first, I sought medical treatment. Doctors would always ask, "Mr. Pearse, do you feel like harming yourself?"

Now, I never wanted to commit suicide, but I would always answer, "If I went to sleep and did not wake up, I was good with that outcome."

I did not want to die; I just had no strong desire live. It took years before one doctor told me that my attitude was not healthy. He was correct. I remember one therapist asked, "What brought you in today?" I told her my story, and it devastated her. I had to comfort her. Her response was one I was familiar with. Many cannot imagine having to deal with such tragedy. I had to console her and reassure her it was going to be okay. After that visit, I stopped going to therapists. I realized I was a little better. I was able to function at work, or at least, I thought I was functioning. Work kept me busy and gave me some motivation to get out of bed. But there was a season of not wanting to move out from the coffin of my covers. Depression from grief is real and, yes, I suffered. One of the things that did help was anti-depressants. Once they were prescribed and I started to take them, I could tell the difference. I'm an advocate for seeking and using medical treatment for healing.

To heal from this, you cannot do it alone. We found a group called Compassionate Friends. This is a group for parents who have lost a child. Attending meetings was instrumental to my healing process. There are times well-intended people just do not understand what you are going through. They often say things to try to help but miss the mark. I also believed that the prayers of the saints of God sustained and carried me through this valley of death I traveled. God's Word was also a great help and was a great part of my healing process. His Word is a living word and will provide comfort and healing. Weeping may endure for a night, but there is a joy that comes. As I read the story of David in 2 Samuel 12:23, it states, "But now he has died. Why should I go without food? Can I bring him to life again? I will go to him, but he will not return to me."

I knew both of my children were believers. They had made a public confession believing in the death, burial, and resurrection of Christ. So, though they are not here with me, I have a hope of seeing and rejoicing with them again. I will go to them. These words and others from the Bible have given me life and hope. God's Word gives me peace and has taken the sting out of their death.

"What a wonderful God we have — he is the Father of our Lord Jesus Christ, the source of every mercy, and the one who so wonderfully comforts and strengthens us in our hardships and trials. And why does he do this? So

"While the child was alive," he said, *"I fasted and wept, thinking,
God might have mercy on me, and the child would live. But now that he's dead, why fast?
Can I bring him back now? I can go to him, but he can't come to me."*
2 Samuel 12: 22-23

that when others are troubled, needing our sympathy and encouragement, we can pass on to them this same help and comfort God has given us." (2 Corinthians 1:3-4)

One of the hardest things for me to do is talk to my wife about our children. Yvette wanted to talk about the children to help her heal. I was unable to do that for her. Talking with her about our children was and still is difficult for me. I have gotten better. Before, I was done after 20 or 30 seconds. I would shut down and disconnect from the conversation. I now can go longer, but it just leaves me with such an empty feeling. I can talk to a stranger or a group of people; I have the strength to do that. Talking to my wife is difficult. The pain and memories are harder with her. There is a connection of a great mutual loss, a hole in the heart that will never be filled, and I know she knows that feeling. I know I cannot fill it; I can only empathize with the loss.

People often say after they suffer a loss, they can look at me and gain strength. I can say it is only by the grace of God. Those who have not had a loss often will say, "I could not endure what you have been through."

All I can say is, "We serve the same God. Believe me, it is not Brian's strength, but the Christ in me. It has been through prayer and God's grace that I have been able to do what you see."

I did realize that I had a platform and voice through telling my story. I do know that some people will listen and take heed. I never wanted this mission, this job, but I have accepted the hand that I have been dealt. Because of my telling my story, some people have changed their behavior and actions and do put on a seatbelt when they ride in a car. My goal is to save a life and prevent injuries that occur with crashes. My children, for some reason, made a bad choice on November 14, 2006, and did not put on a seatbelt. This resulted in their being ejected from the car, costing them their lives. I want to spare others the grief, agony, and pain I endured. No parent wants to bury their child; it is not the natural order of life.

In memory of Kiara and Jameel, my wife and I established the K & J Foundation. Its mission is to save lives and prevent injuries. To date we have awarded 17 educational scholarships to graduating high school seniors. Also, we have made numerous presentations on the importance of wearing a seatbelt. There are times when I do not think I tell my story enough, especially when I hear of a youth in the community who was in a crash and died because he or she was not wearing a seatbelt. I think a life may have been saved had they been wearing one. Motor vehicle crashes continue to be the No. 1 cause of death for teenagers. Some of these deaths are preventable.

In Philippians 2: 20-24, Paul is debating with himself whether it is better for him to live or die. For in death he would be with Christ. I have flirted with the same notion — living or dying, which one is better for me? My reasons may not have been as virtuous as his. I was escaping misfortune and misery. In the end, he concluded it was better for him to live and do more fruitful work. I will do the same — live and do a fruitful work. Nothing I do will bring Kiara and Jameel back to me in this life, but I can go to them in the next life. I will continue to tell the story and honor them so others may live.

Brian Pearse was born in Queens, N.Y., in December 1960. He joined the USAF in 1984, served 20 years, and was honorably discharged in 2004. He retired in Mississippi. Brian currently is youth minister at First Missionary Baptist Church in Gulfport, Miss. He is owner of Brian Pearse Photography and is founder and director of K&J Foundation.

Chapter sponsored by K&J Foundation and State Farm

CHAPTER 3

Beyond the Obstacles

By Dr. Valerie Arthur

I was still thinking of my recent luxurious Royal Caribbean vacation cruise as I entered the lobby of the Smith Family Foundation, a private grant-making institution, founded in Trenton, N.J., in 2016. On the lobby wall hung our core values: education, cultivation, transformation, and urban ministry. I am the urban ministry director and foundation board chair. Sharrar, the receptionist, greeted me with a smile, "Good morning, Dr. Arthur, welcome back. How was your vacation? Mrs. Nunnally would like to see you in her office before morning briefing."

What could possibly be so important before coffee? Did I forget to complete an assignment before I left? What could have possibly been of such urgency that she had to see me first thing? I had a feeling that the outcome of our pending conversation was not going to be favorable. Hurriedly, I put my belongings away, grabbed myself a cup of strong coffee, and made my way up to the third floor.

"Dr. Arthur, come on in. Take a seat. Let's sit at the conference table and talk," Mrs. Nunnally said. I have known this young lady all her life; her pleasant tone, and shy, girlish smile was not fooling me. She wanted something. I was not giving in this time. I was going to firmly stand my ground. "Welcome back. How was your trip? Did you have a nice time? Are you glad to be back?"

"Enough with the pleasantries, Mrs. Nunnally. How can I help you?"

She proceeded to say, "Dr. Arthur" — a signal to my brain that I was not going to like what she was going to say next. "Dr. Arthur, I really need for you to go to Haiti for me."

Instantly, a memory began to formulate of the lady with the big, poofy, pink hair whom I had seen on TV many years before: Jan Crouch. She and her husband, Paul, were the founders of Trinity Broadcasting Networks.

Many years had passed since that one, rare Saturday night that I happened to come across their annual telethon. Jan was seeking sponsors to support her Smile of a Child Foundation Haiti initiative. They were proposing to build a $2 million medical facility in Port-au-Prince, Haiti. Jan's pink hair and face were images I associated with the word Haiti.

As Mrs. Nunnally continued talking, I could hear Jan Crouch's sweet little bubbly voice telling the story about a child. The memory still haunted her: "I remember picking him up off the cement floor and holding him in my arms.

As I was holding him," she said, "all I could say was, 'Jesus loves you.' I kept repeating, 'Jesus loves you.' Moments later, he quit breathing and died in my arms." She went on to say, "One day, children will not have to die on cement floors. They will be able to receive medical care for what we here in America consider curable diseases." I was so moved by Jan's compelling testimony that I did something I had never done before. I made a $100 donation.

Interrupting my thoughts, Mrs. Nunnally repeated her question, "So, will you go?"

"Go where?" I asked.

"To Saint-Michel de l'Attalaye. It's in the mountain region of Haiti."

I responded, "Go to Haiti? Why do you want me to go to Haiti? Only medical people go to Haiti. I am a theologian not a medical doctor. Sorry, the answer is no!"

Apparently, she had donated $5,000 to help a local church finish a water well and was considering making a private donation to help build a school.

"I really want to help, but I cannot leave the foundation right now," I said.

"I need your help," she countered.

I asked, "When do you want me to go, Mrs. Nunnally?"

"This Friday!" she said.

"Just so that I am clear on what you are asking me, if I am to understand you correctly, you want me to go to the mountains of Haiti to a place that no one has ever heard of before, to report if a water well has a pump and if there is a need for a new school. And you want me to leave on Friday?"

She responded, "Yes!"

Smiling to myself and at her, I replied: "I don't think so, Mrs. Nunnally. I have no desire to go to Haiti; I do not feel the leading of the Lord to go to the mountains of Haiti. Haiti is not a ministry I wish to pursue. Sorry! My answer is no!"

Suddenly, without warning, her whole facial expression changed from the chief executive officer of the Smith Family Foundation to that of my pouting, whining little sister.

"Val, I am your little sister. Please, you are the oldest, and your little sister needs your help. Please go for me. You know how Mommy feels about helping children. Think about the children, about all the lives that could possibly be transformed because of this one little trip."

Sister or no sister, chief executive officer or not, I was determined not to go to Haiti. As I was thinking of another word for no, again I heard the meek voice of the woman with the poofy pink hair. It was as if she were looking directly at me through the lens of the television camera, pleading to my compassion: "Will you help us? Will you donate today? Will you put a smile on a child's face today? Will you contribute to Smile of a Child in Haiti?"

Is it possible that Jesus was faced with this same dilemma in Matthew 15 when his compassion heard a cry from a place of darkness? The cry of a desperate Canaanite mother whose child was being exploited by insalubrious men. "... Lord, Son of David, have mercy on me!" "... Lord, help me!" A call to the compassion of Christ. "Have mercy on me, O Lord, thou Son of David; my daughter is grievously vexed with a devil."

The compassion of Christ was willing; however, there were obstacles prohibiting him from responding. But He answered her not a word. And His disciples came and besought Him, saying, "Send her away, for she crieth after us." But He answered and said, "I am not sent but unto the lost sheep of the house of Israel." Then came she and worshiped him, saying, "Lord, help me." But He answered and said, "It is not meet to take the children's bread and to cast it to dogs." And she said, "Truth, Lord: yet the dogs eat of the crumbs which fall from their masters' table." Then Jesus answered and said unto her, "O, Woman, great is thy faith. Be it unto thee even as thou wilt." And her daughter was made whole from that very hour.

What was Jesus' reasoning in hesitating to answer her; why did he remain silent? Did he stop to consider the obstacles, to send her away as requested by the disciples? The obstacle of being out of time, perhaps: "I am not sent but unto the lost sheep of the house."

How would I answer. Would I answer? Was I hearing this same sense of desperation in the voice of Jan Crouch? Would my compassion find a way to extended itself beyond the Urban Centers of America, as Jesus had, to reach a people I did not know, to travel two and half hours off the coastline of Florida to foreign lands? Was Jesus actually considering sending me to people crying after him, "Lord help us?" Was I to be one of the ones the Lord would use to answer the call, "Lord, help! Lord, help … ." Had he found a way to use me beyond my obstacles?

My two traveling companions, Dawn Reyes, the foundation's community engagement specialist, and Evangelist Matias Rojas, arrived at Cap-Haïtien International Airport at 9 a.m. on August 12, 2016. The moment I stepped off the plane into the 80-degree humid weather, I knew I was not prepared for what awaited me on the other side of the terminal. According to the informational article I read on the plane, Cap-Haïtien is located in the northern region of Haiti. Le Cap, as it is also known, was founded by the French in 1670. The luxurious beaches and five-star hotels have enhanced Cap-Haïtien's reputation as being the most sought-after vacation spot for the Haitian upper class.

Walking through the terminal we could hear the sounds of the local musicians as they sang and played the steel drums, buleador, and the maracas. We retrieved our luggage, exited the airport, and met our host, Pastor Jean David Jean, who was waiting at the curbside.

Pastor Jean, senior pastor and founder of Victory Tabernacle Church and administrator of the School of Flowers, is an English-speaking, 30-year-old, tall, thin, handsome, smooth, dark-skinned man. During our time together, I learned that he had recently returned to Saint-Michel de l'Attalaye after spending 10 years receiving a biblical degree in Santo-Domingo, Dominican Republic. He and his lovely wife, Rosie, hosted us in their home, acted as tour guides, historians, and drivers.

I was at a loss for words to properly describe what I witnessed as we left the beaches of Cap-Haïtien behind to make the seven-hour drive up the mountainous region of Michel-de-l'Attalaye, Artibonite. At times I found it hard to breathe, not because of the air quality, but because of what my eyes were beholding. I could not and still cannot paint a picture of the extreme poverty that draped the landscape of such a beautiful, colorful country. It has been five years since my first trip, and I am still overwhelmed with the inhumane living conditions of some of my Haitian sisters and brothers.

Non-governmental agencies, missionaries, and medical volunteers also have not been able to adequately describe the desolation they, too, experienced before and after the 2010 earthquake. Some wrote that it was a nation devastated by the appearance of war. They described collapsed buildings; the disregarded, decayed human remains that became a cesspool for the feasting of supersized rats; the air polluted with black smoke because of the chemicals released from the continuous burning of rubber tires in protest of the corruption of the Haitian government; the naked orphan children who roamed the streets looking for food at the market garbage dump; the consistent disruption of daily life attributed to gang and political violence; homelessness, starvation, the lack of medical treatment — just a total and complete destruction and devastation of an already oppressive system.

Arriving in Saint-Michel de l'Attalaye at dusk, we decided it was best to visit the school the next day. When we finally made our way to the school, arriving at 8 a.m., we found approximately thirty elementary school-aged children sitting patiently waiting underneath a blue shred tarp tacked to six pine tree poles. The benches they sat on were made out of various pieces of scrap wood. Some of the shoe-less children had walked five miles to sit under the tarp. Without paper or pencil they eagerly responded to the church volunteer who could barely read himself. I stood there dumbfounded, hearing the plea of the Canaanite woman, the voice of Jan Crouch: "Son of David, help me. Will you help us bring a smile to a child today?" I answered not a word. There were obstacles. I was the obstacle.

Classical seminary training does not prepare one for this. Frankly, I had never even thought about such ministry. I wanted to preach and teach in large stadiums, on football fields, in seminaries at Bible colleges. I never really expected my Christian faith to require me to go beyond teaching Jesus to becoming like Jesus. How would I represent Jesus under such circumstances? What could I possibly say to this community, these children born in the 21st century but not of the 21st century, children who went home to the normalcy of clay, two-room, dirt-floor houses without electricity, without inside bathrooms or clean drinking water? What would I, a privileged American but a person of limited means and resources do differently from the religious and nonprofit organizations that came before me? The world has invested billions of dollars and other resources into Haiti, yet according to the Global Finance News Report, Haiti still is the poorest country in the Western Hemisphere and the thirteenth poorest country in the world. Money was not the solution to the problem, neither was the mere teaching of the attributes of Jesus. I had long come to the conclusion that folks were tired of hearing about Jesus; they needed to see a manifestation of Jesus. I would write my report as promised, fulfilling my assignment, and go back to my life.

"And she said, 'Truth, Lord' yet the dogs eat of the crumbs which fall from their master's table."
Matthew 15:27

On our 25-minute drive back to the pastor's house, I had a chance to reflect on the core values of the Smith Family Foundation: education, transformation, cultivation and urban ministry. The poor children of Haiti were no different from the poor children of America; they deserve the chance at life, liberty, and the pursuit of happiness. Both were in need of opportunities. Is not education an opportunity? And that is one of the things we do best at the Smith Family Foundation: open doors to opportunities. However, opportunities come with obstacles; thus, living out my faith to truly be like Jesus meant I had to create an opportunity to walk into this new experience of Christ's compassion, accept the paradigm shift taking form in my thinking, and overcome the obstacle of the Smith Family Foundation's commitment to only provide educational opportunities to the residents of the city of Trenton N.J. After all, it was Mrs. Nunnally, the CEO, who sent me to Haiti on a fact-finding mission.

My first plan of action was to appeal to the educators of our board members. The school system in Haiti is a for-profit system that remains in shambles after the 2010 earthquake, which damaged or destroyed the majority of schools. Literacy rates hover around 55 percent for both sexes, and most of the 15,200 primary schools are community run or funded by religious institutions. As a result, the poor remain in a cycle of poverty without a clear path to attaining an education. Those children fortunate enough to afford school are still at a disadvantage because the official medium of education is Creole. An unfortunate effect, trapping the children of the poor in a vicious cycle of ongoing poverty, because the children must know French in order to pass the certificate examination at the end of grade five. When they enroll in high school, they find chaos waiting for them, especially in rural schools, where teachers are ill-prepared, and materials are inadequate.

Today, the school we founded, Katherine School of Flowers, located in Saint-Michel de l'Attalaye, is one of a very few schools in Haiti that is totally free to children in poor rural communities. In its short five years of existence, it has grown from 30 children to educating 220 children, providing a free education to those who cannot afford to attend private or government schools. The school provides a feeding program, soccer field, 18 paid staff members, and an adult education program. We are in the process of building a middle school and beginning a fundraising effort for a technical high school. We also offer technical support, leadership development, and teachers' training to other schools in the surrounding areas.

My second plan of action was to appeal to the business-owner board members. The opportunities of free education are impactful; however, they alone do not stabilize a community. The availability of employment adds value and self-worth to a person's life. Through many community conversations and religious services, Black Gold International SA, a Haitian company, was born. Primarily a farming company, Black Gold employs approximately 40 people; they are the parents of our students or those who have graduated from our adult education program. Our vision is to be entrusted to feed the nation of Haiti by using the best practices in agricultural production.

Last, but not least, an appeal was made to the only theologian on the board — me. I had to change the way that I think. The gospel is not only to be preached behind the four walls of a church or taught in a seminary. I had to ask myself what the "Great Commission" looks like in my life, how loudly I can live my faith. Surprisingly, it does not involve building a church building.

Christ Centered in the City, my personal ministry, has been afforded the opportunities to develop and conduct leadership development training with religious leaders in Haiti. Our focus is not only to preach salvation and attributes of Christ, but also to create environmental construction workers.

Proverbs 23:7 states, "For as he thinketh in his heart, so is he." In Haiti, there is systemic poverty and poor quality of life, because somewhere in that society, someone has a poor thought process. My commission at this time is to render assistance in thinking about thinking, to become a person to change and construct their own environments. Me, living my faith out loud.

Dr. Valerie Arthur is a founding member of the Smith Family Foundation of New Jersey, where she currently serves as the board chair and director of urban ministry. She is also founder of Christ Centered in the City International Ministries, and host of Christ Centered in the City Café. She served the New Jersey Department of Corrections for 30 years, retiring as the first African American administrator of the 100-year-old Edna Mahon Correctional facility for Women, the only women's prison in the state of New Jersey. Dr. Arthur is an ordained elder of Mt. Sinai Holy Church of America Incorporated; she is currently assigned to Calvary Pentecostal Church, located in Trenton N.J., where she serves as assistant to her pastor and Christian education coordinator.

She completed her undergraduate education from Carin University and received both a master of divinity and doctor of ministry degree (prison, policy and transformative justice) from New Brunswick Theological Seminary.

CHAPTER 4

Preserved for Purpose

By Dr. Shamara Byrd

After hitting the snooze button three times, I knew it was time for me to start the dreadful daily 5 a.m. routine of getting ready for high school. I dragged myself out of bed and stumbled to the bathroom. As I washed my face, the heat from the water gave me my first dose of energy. The telephone rang, interrupting my journey. Gripped by fear, I ran to the phone. No good news ever came that early in the morning. Only heartache and death were on the other end of my line.

"Hello," I said, reluctantly and nervously.

"Shamara, can you bring me some clothes? My mom kicked me out."

Although I heard the question, my brain wasn't working at full capacity that early in the morning. It took a moment to recognize that it was my friend Chanel.

"Did you hear me? I need you." Her voice sounded urgent and scared.

"Okay, I'm on my way."

"Hurry … please."

There was no time to ask questions, no time to finish my morning routine. I moved quickly, packing a pair of jeans, a shirt, and a pair of shoes. I quickly brushed my teeth, swirled a little Listerine in my mouth, and threw on a wrinkled t-shirt and jeans before darting for the door. Chanel lived down the block, so I ran toward her house. The sound of her voice rang in my ear and pushed me to keep going, even though my chest burned, and I had a stitch in my side. I wasn't sure how to feel. What kind of mother would put her child out, especially at five in the morning? Anger at her mother and fear over my concern for Chanel's safety battled for space in my spirit.

As I approached, I wasn't sure what I was going to find. I glanced over the porch and yard, but there was no sign of Chanel. Was this girl playing a joke on me? Then from the bushes a soft voice whispered, "Over here." Chanel's hand waved from behind the bush. As she emerged, I couldn't believe what I was seeing. Chanel was dressed in only a black body suit. She stood there with her arms folded, shuffling on the balls of her feet to fight off the cold.

We didn't speak as she quickly took the bag of clothes and returned to the bushes to get dressed. Tears ran down my face, and I watched her walk away. When she emerged, she looked like a normal high school student. We walked to the bus stop and waited in silence. It wasn't until we were sitting on the bus that I noticed the blue and purples bruises. "Hell, no! Are you okay?"

"I'm okay," Her body language suggested she was used to hiding the pain. As we rode, I tried to get her to tell me about why she was put out. She didn't go into much detail, and simply shared that her mom and sister always treated her badly and did things to her.

My mind went to the bruises that often marred her caramel-colored skin. She always gave some crazy excuse. I asked if they came from her mom and sister, and she said yes. I was a river of tears. I wanted to hold her and tell her everything would be okay. I wanted to stop her pain, keep her safe and protected, because I knew her pain oh, so well. The pain of being abused and rejected by those who are supposed to love and protect you.

Like Chanel, I, too, understood the pain of feeling unloved and unprotected. Her tears reminded me of the many tears I cried after my parents divorced. The agony of watching my daddy move on and create another family that did not include me scarred my soul for decades to come. As if my heart wasn't broken enough, I was molested by a family member and endured a short season of homelessness. My cry for my daddy fell on deaf ears. My former hero never called or came to check on his baby girl. "What did I do wrong? Why does he not love me anymore?" were questions I desperately sought answers to, but my attempts were unsuccessful. At that moment, I felt like a daddy-less daughter, dropped by the very one who was supposed to affirm my beauty, self-worth, and teach me how I should be treated as a woman. I was left to live with the unresolved feelings as a child, which manifested in my adult life and relationships.

As time passed, I would see bruises on Chanel's body, and they made me think of my bruised soul. We both had our secrets, and we lived behind the mask. We graduated, and although we lost touch, I held Chanel in my heart and that memory in my head. She was a manifestation of me, a reflection of all my pain and insecurities. So, when it was time to declare a major, I chose social work. I wanted to help all the Chanel's of the world. To give them the support they need in a safe space to confront and conquer their pain.

Over the years, I often wondered about Chanel. Then one day, Ding! That was the sound of my Facebook messenger notification. Much to my surprise, it was my long-lost childhood friend. I was ecstatic to hear from her. I had often wondered about her. As if that weren't emotional enough for me, the words I began to read brought tears to my eyes.

"I am forever appreciative for how you intervened in my life when we were growing up. You are special and unique, and I just wanted you to know that I treasured your involvement in my life! Keep smiling."

Can I say I need two boxes of tissue? Not only did she surprise me, her words touched my soul. As a teenager, I had no clue that I was being prepared to give birth to the passion and purpose that was inside me. She was exactly right. As I cried, I was smiling with joy on the inside.

As I look in the rear-view mirror of my life, before I welcomed Jesus into my life, I was a spiritually dead person living in darkness. I lived in bondage to the strongholds of low self-confidence, self-doubt, rejection, abandonment, and fear of failure. I was merely existing instead of living. No joy. No peace. No purpose. I spent many years chasing love and affirmation from the wrong man. When all along, I was unconditionally loved by the one and only man. Once I fully understood God's plan of salvation, accepted Christ as my Lord and Savior, I found a joy that can never be taken away from me. I discovered a level of peace that is unable to be explained, and in time, the Holy Spirit revealed the very things I was created to do in the kingdom. With prayer, the help of the Holy Spirit, godly wisdom, and an inner determination, I was able to overcome the trauma from my past and soared like an eagle into my destiny. Through all the hurt and disappointment, I encountered along the path to purpose, God preserved me.

God has allowed me to be light to women who are in darkness and this led me to start Byrd's Nest Outreach, Inc., a non-profit, and The DIVA Academy, a for-profit business. Both have the goal of supporting women who are broken from trials of life, bound to the stronghold of the enemy, bankrupt in their faith, and blind to the power of God. They provide biblical principles and strategies to help them learn to love their imperfect self through a perfect Savior, grow into confident and courageous women, and build mutually edifying relationships with like-minded women.

Overcoming anything is a process. Is it an easy process? Absolutely not! Will there be days when you feel like quitting the process? You bet! Will there be days when you cry and question God's love and sovereignty? No doubt! But endure your process.

Often, it can seem like our pain is purposeless. As we try our best to tackle the problems we deal with day in and day out, it is in those moments when we must remember the words found in Jeremiah 29:11: God knows the plans He has for each of us. It's never just to hurt us. It's never just to disappoint us. It's never just to make us feel alone or forgotten. It's never just to break us. It's never just to humiliate us. Though the process is filled with mountain-and-valley experiences, trust the Lord and lean not on our own limited understanding. God does not make mistakes. He is sovereign and omniscient. He knows the plans He has for you. Plans to prosper you and not harm you. Our Creator, God the Father, knows just how much we can handle before we are destroyed. He will preserve and protect our mind and faith as our spiritual gifts and natural talents are developed and we are fully prepared to walk in purpose as a vessel, modeling the character of Christ.

Dr. Shamara L. Byrd was born and raised in the inner city of Miami, Fla. She holds a bachelor's and master's degree in social work, an educational specialist's degree in educational leadership and exceptional student

education, and a doctorate degree in ministry with a concentration in Christian counseling.

Dr. Byrd has over 26 years of experience as a K-12 teacher, school social worker, school administrator, and adjunct college professor. She founded Byrd's Nest Outreach, Inc., a faith-based 501(c)3 recognized, nonprofit organization whose mission is to reduce homelessness among single mothers with school-aged children. Dr. Byrd is also the owner of The D.I.V.A. (Determined Individual with a Victorious Attitude) Coaching Academy, LLC, which provides women of faith with skills and biblically based strategies to identify and confront self-defeating thoughts and behaviors that prevent them from living a life of peace, purpose, and prosperity.

CHAPTER 5

Faith Heals Shattered Trust

By Regina Addison

As children we all believed that our parents and those who were older than we were would protect us from things that were a threat to who we were and to whom we would become. We looked at them with all that we understood love to be, and we trusted them blindly because we felt protected in their presence. There was nothing in our makeup that said we shouldn't or couldn't trust them, and the bigger they were, the more protection we felt. We walked past them with the confidence of knowing we had nothing to worry about and nothing to fear — until the ones we trusted most became our greatest fear.

Home became a place of unfamiliar acts that became very familiar as the years passed. A part of me knew the acts were wrong, but the adults who initiated and engaged in these acts tried to convince me that they were normal. No matter how young a person is, he or she knows something about these acts does not seem normal, and nothing about them feels right.

After each act, the adult told me, "This is our little secret," but all the while I knew that it wasn't a secret I wanted to keep. I wanted to shout it from the rooftop, to put it in a bottle and send it out to sea. I wanted to blow the whistle and sound the alarm because I wanted it to stop. But with every "THIS IS OUR LITTLE SECRET" came a threat of "IF YOU TELL ANYBODY, I'LL _____."

I don't know what your threat was, but mine varied from getting a beating to being killed. The idea of familiar hands touching unfamiliar places plagued my entire childhood. It wasn't until I was 16 and pregnant that I knew I had to take a stand. I had to do for my child the one thing no one did for me: I had to protect her. She was the one person on earth who had to love me without prejudice or choice. I was all she had, and she was all I had. I was lost, and I was alone, but having her growing inside me changed my outlook on love and life. Rape and molestation were the situations I faced time and time again; fear was the obstacle that stood in my way, but my love for the life growing inside of me was reason enough to take a stand.

I found myself in my closet with a Bible and a prayer.

"God, if there is a God, I need you to help me, because if you don't, I'm going to die right here."

Before Christ, I thought that every bad thing that could happen did happen, and there was no one who cared. I believed that I had no purpose and

---

never thought there was a plan for my life. I actually believed I was placed on this earth for men and women alike to take advantage of me. I was young, and I wasn't even sure that God existed, and if he did exist, I was pretty sure he wasn't concerned about me; I mean how could he be? How could I believe that there was a God sitting high, looking low, and allowing these things to happen to someone at such a young age? How could such a loving God allow this curve ball to be thrown at me? There was no way that God could see me; there was definitely something blocking his view of the happenings of my life.

After finding that God did exist, I would later conclude that not only did He care, but He was there; not only did He see, but He knew. God heard my prayers, and He's still hearing my prayers. When I took the time to talk to Him and to listen, He began to give me direction. I was surprised to know that He was truly a friend of mine, and that He was concerned about every milestone, every curve ball, and every predicament.

My experience in this arena of life taught me to pray differently and created a passion and burning desire in me to help others. I told my Creator, "God, if you take away the hurt and the sting of all the things I've had to endure, I will reach back and help others. I will make sure that no one I know or come in contact with will ever have to suffer alone the way I did."

It is my purpose, my passion, and my plan to make everyone feel like someone in my presence. God has blessed me with several ministries to be an encouragement to others. Monday through Friday I send out words of encouragement (Keys of the Kingdom) on a phone line. Every Monday evening, I do a live broadcast, "Keys of the Kingdom," where I share real-life experiences and how God has, through His word, given us the ability to overcome.

Your situation, condition, or circumstance may not be rape or molestation, but I do know that pain of any caliber still hurts. I want you to be encouraged in knowing that there is NOTHING you have experienced or will ever experience that is about you. Yes, you are the one going through it. Yes, you are the one who has to seek God for an exit strategy. Yes, you are the one who is feeling the effects of it, but everything you have endured or will endure is for a testimony unto others. Someone somewhere is waiting to hear your testimony. Someone somewhere is waiting to hear about how God kept you. Someone somewhere needs to know how God brought you out. Someone somewhere needs to know how God covered you by His grace. Someone somewhere is waiting on you to make it through. Don't let fear hold you back, but let love prevail. God hears your prayers, and although there are times you may feel lonely, you are never alone. In your darkest hours and in your weakest moments, the light and strength of God is present. That's why you're still here; that's why you haven't given up. No matter what you've been through, no matter what you go through, you still have worth, and you still have purpose.

Regina Addison leads several ministries. She operates a phone line, Keys of the Kingdom, through which she encourages others. She also conducts a weekly Keys of the Kingdom broadcast where she shares real-life experiences and shows how God gives the ability to overcome.

Regina Addison (Abisheba) is the second born of four children and was raised in an impoverished neighborhood. At a very young age, she developed a relationship with Christ. She grew up in a dysfunctional family and is an abuse survivor. She is a mother of three and a minister of the gospel. She is the host of Keys of the Kingdom, a Facebook live feed that is broadcast every Monday night. She also presents words of encouragement via phone each week, Monday through Friday.

CHAPTER 6

Brush with Death Brings New Life

By Jean Turner

I was in the prime of my life! I was a career girl in a man's world, a world where women were breaking barriers, creating their own paths, and doing some dope things in spite of the "good ol' boys" mentality that continues to reside within the ranks. I fell prey to the lifestyle. I got caught up in the success of my army career, the next rank, and the next best position. I based my goals on what I wanted with no regard for God's plan and purpose for me. For many years I wandered in the wilderness. But in the blink of an eye, my life changed. Suddenly! Unexpectedly! I went from being this healthy, "HOOAH, HOOAH" army chick and marathon runner to chemotherapy in zero to five seconds! The side effects that resulted from nine months of chemotherapy caused me to go into congestive heart failure. Exactly nine weeks from the day that I got to ring the bell signifying my final chemotherapy treatment, I went into cardiac arrest! One moment I was sitting up in a wheelchair in the emergency room and the next thing I knew, I was waking up in a hospital bed with all sorts of tubes connected to me, monitors, and a big, scary-looking machine surrounding my bedside. It looked like a large fortress. Unbeknownst to me, the doctors told my husband and family that my heart was beating at 1% and that they did not expect me to make it past the next few hours. I later found out that one of the doctor's exact words to my husband was, "She is going to die!"

I underwent several surgeries. When my heart function began to show signs of improvement, I began to regain consciousness. I remember being so weak that my nurses had to bathe and reposition me. I remember being unable to move any part of my body other than my fingers. As a nurse, I knew that something bad had happened to me. My mind kept going back to the night I went to the emergency room, but no matter how much I tried, I couldn't remember a thing. I knew the road to recovery after chemotherapy was going to take some time. I remember looking forward to regaining my life back afterwards. I wanted to be normal again. I wanted to go back to work. I wanted to be able to race again. I loved to travel. Our last major vacation was in 2017, so I was looking forward to a tropical change of scenery. But no one or nothing could have prepared me for this. Here I was again in a serious battle for my life!

A few days after I regained consciousness, I was transferred out of the intensive care unit to the heart recovery unit. I was stable and out of immediate danger, but my heart rate remained elevated. I was still unable to move any part of my body without assistance. What you do not use, you lose. I had been in that ICU bed for close to a month, and my muscles began to atrophy. I was unable to scoot over to the side of the bed, let alone raise myself up from the bed and stand without someone holding me up. I was immediately transferred to an inpatient rehabilitation center to receive what I needed to regain the strength and ability to stand, walk, bathe, and dress myself.

The cancer diagnosis and chemotherapy took me on a spiritual journey. It was during this time that I learned to lean on and depend on God. No one else had the power to bring me through that. I learned to be transparent with God. I literally had conversations with Him as I lay in my bed recovering in between treatments. I spent many days reading my Bible. I found out that in Him I live, move, and have my being. His strength is in me — the strength to be resilient, the strength to overcome, the strength of the warrior soldier that the army trained me to be during all my years of service. I spoke His word over my life. I told myself that God did not bring me this far to leave me now. That same warrior spirit raised up, and I remember saying to myself, "I will not die in this place!"

I grew up in church and accepted Christ when I was growing up. I rededicated my life to Him years later, but at some point in my career, I found myself walking aimlessly in the wilderness. I still loved God, but I had goals. Even in the midst of these back-to-back health challenges, He never failed to show me that He was still there with me.

I am so in awe of God's faithfulness! He is faithful to the promises in His word. I am so happy that He allowed me to be a living testimony. I thought about staying in the army for a few more years once I recovered from chemotherapy, but that was not God's plan for me. This entire experience has caused me to re-evaluate my priorities and focus on what is most important: God and family. Everything else falls into place when we make Him our number-one priority.

Many people work so hard to obtain a certain level of success but fail to do what is necessary to maintain it. It is hard to be successful when you are sick and unhealthy. There is so much work to be done. We overcome by the word of our testimony, our story. God is using my testimony, my experiences and knowledge to help others overcome their health obstacles and ultimately practice stewardship over their health. A person's current state of health impacts his or her prognosis (chance of survival) and recovery. The same doctors who worked to resuscitate me in the emergency room almost two years ago are the same ones who look at me now and say, "If you had not been in such great shape, we would not be having this conversation." We know that God is the healer, but he orchestrated the plan to have these same doctors on duty and in position when I arrived.

We do not know what will transpire from one moment to the next. I woke up one morning and ended up coding in someone's emergency room a few hours later. The time is now! Now is the time to get in formation and line up with what God has for you. Do not be like me and wait for something drastic to happen for Him to get your attention. If you are unsure about what you are supposed to be doing, ask Him. Make Him and His will your priority. When you do, He will guide you in the right direction.

As for me, what once was is now new.

Now I am living my best life and living my faith out loud through The Spirit of a Warrior Life Enterprises, LLC, which I founded as a result of my journey through cancer and treatment. I minister to others through my holistic health nurse coaching and education company. Through my own testament of faith, I help others to draw on their innate strength to overcome obstacles and ultimately learn to practice stewardship over their health so they can be fit to do all that God has ordained them to do.

Jean Turner is an author, speaker, certified holistic health coach, and CEO of The Spirit of a Warrior Life Enterprises, LLC, created to help others draw on their innate strength to overcome, reclaim their lives, and live them to the fullest, as God intended. Under her business umbrella, she uses the mediums of podcasting (Health Chat w/Coach Jean), self-care and non-fiction books, and mini-workbooks to accompany her signature wellness programs, affording every opportunity for her clients to receive the highest results intended. Tenured in the nursing vocation for over 30 years, Jean empowers both her patients and clients to take charge of their health: body, mind, and spirit.

CHAPTER 7

Bold Faith, Beyond the Numbers

By Denise Howell

I was five years old when I met Jesus and entered into a relationship with Him. I was an only child born into a family of addiction and abuse. Jesus walked with me through my adolescence, spending time with me, loving on me, and being a companion. I have heard of many children of abuse having tangible encounters with Jesus. I was one of those children. He would come to comfort me frequently when I was a child. In addition to tangible encounters with Jesus, I also experienced miraculous healing as early as the age of 13. The first healing I recall, I had been studying in church about the healing power of Jesus. On the way home from school, I had taken a shortcut and was bitten by a dog. Reversing my route and taking the long way home, I kept asking Jesus to take the pain away and heal my leg. He did. The doctors at the emergency room almost reported my mom for neglect, because the wound had three days of new tissue growth. I kept telling the doctors that my Jesus healed my leg! I had told my mom not to take me to the hospital. That was my first real-live witnessing experience that I recall.

There's a very important point I need you to understand. I do not "believe" in God; I know He is real and alive. I do not simply believe the Word, I know that it is truth. I have spent many hours with Him, and He has done many miracles in my life. The Word has come alive in my life too many times to count. Now, the Word is manifested in my life daily. But that is another story for another day. Today, I want to tell you about how I live my faith out loud. It was my Sunday School teacher who introduced me to Jesus. Many years later, after years of my own addiction and a desperate search for that love I felt only with Jesus, I accepted Him as my Lord and Savior. I was 22. Then, after many trials and tribulations, I surrendered and dedicated my life to Him when I was 43.

Though I have been walking with Jesus most of my life, it was not until God led me, at the age of 48, to start a public accounting business that I felt free to speak boldly about my faith. Of course, I have always given my testimony whenever someone at church would ask or when someone learning about this thing called salvation would ask about my relationship with God. Those are the "safe" times of witnessing. It was not until He put me in the position to counsel people in this public accounting business that I truly started living my faith out loud. After all, this was His business, not mine or any other man's. Through the business, God sends people to me daily to receive His instruction, direction, encouragement, warnings, and guidance. Most of the time, they believe they are coming to receive professional services. It's really cool to see their reaction when I speak answers regarding questions they have been seeking about things I could not possibly have known about.

That's when they know it's God speaking to them. In the beginning, it took a bold leap of faith to speak the words that were persisting to be spoken that, to me, seemed random and completely off topic. But, once I got the courage to speak these seemingly random words, I found that they were God's words. The person's reaction let me know that it was from God. Once I got comfortable with speaking God's words, I learned to discern when it was from God. If the words keep pressing to be spoken, I know it's God. The more I witnessed to people, the more God used me. There's a boldness I now have. I have learned that this is my calling. To be God's hands and voice to encourage, love, and strengthen people.

I have always given my testimony whenever someone at church would ask or when someone learning about this thing called salvation would ask about my relationship with God. Those are the "safe" times of witnessing. It was not until He put me in the position to counsel people in this public accounting business that I truly started living my faith out loud.

A woman once came into my office to prepare a non-profit annual return. During our meeting, many ideas came into my mind, and I relayed them to her. She was in awe. She had been searching for months for resolutions to these issues. The ideas that came into my head were completely off the topic of what we were discussing. In fact, the thoughts were so pressing to be spoken, I believe I interrupted her to say them. She left with a contact and to-do list that would keep her busy for months. The annual report became an afterthought to us. This operational information given to her was much more urgent.

Another woman came in as a referral from an existing client. As we were discussing her and her husband's business, an urgent warning came pouring out of my mouth. She was taken aback, since the business opportunity had seemingly fallen into their lap. It was almost too good to be true. I beseeched her to seek legal counsel to create an iron-clad agreement with this "knight in shining armor." She left my office completely confused and discouraged. She discussed the conversation with her husband. I'm not sure of any actions they took from this odd warning. However, a month later she called to get their extension filed, and I was unavailable. When I returned her call, she was dazed. She had just found out that the "knight in shining armor" had somehow removed her and her husband from the bank accounts and the business entity. Luckily, he had not obtained any proprietary information. Not always do people heed God's warnings. But, we must try to stay emotionally unattached so that we can continue to receive God's words.

One of my pastors relates the communication line from God to a radio station on an old AM dial. You have to keep the signal finely tuned to hear a clear message. We must keep all the "static" out of our lives — the static of the world and its beliefs, the static that causes emotion to distort our perspective. The static of our own beliefs or opinions about a situation. We must keep our minds clear and alert. This is done by staying in the Word and meeting with God every morning; by seeking His face daily and asking for His wisdom and knowledge to do His will; by asking God to use you, use your hands to touch, and use your mouth to speak His truth; by praying without ceasing throughout the day; by constantly calling on Him to help you in the moment. I challenge you to find your calling, then to seek God daily, to surrender your life to Him. Really surrender. Living your faith out loud is not for the faint of heart. But, praise God, He will give you strength. His strength. And through His strength, we can do ALL things.

Denise Howell is a CPA who operates a practice that God led her to start in 2013. She is used by God in advising people in His will and helping them to achieve their goals. Denise leads by example and shows people how to live a surrendered life. She is very transparent in her walk with God, genuinely loves everyone with the love of Jesus, and is an encourager. Church and community service play big roles in her life. At church she serves on the production team. In the community, she shares her personal and professional experiences to support organizations that help the homeless, abused, and less advantaged people.

CHAPTER 8

Walk by Faith

By Liz Hoop

It was May 2004. I had arrived home from work and was outside with my husband having an adult beverage as we did every evening, when he said to me, "I'm not meant to be married." That statement felt like a punch in my gut and shattered my heart. I had given 13 years of my life to this man whom I loved.

The process of marital separation began, and I realized I needed to make a change in my life. I was not living for God, and definitely not living it in a way that is pleasing to Him.

Growing up in a minister's home, I knew who God was and knew what faith was all about, having seen my parents living it out and trusting God. But along life's journey, I took a turn, a turn that had taken me down a path of reckless living, with drugs and alcohol, and broken relationships, until one day, a week after my husband's statement, I was on a cold call from work (I worked in outside sales) and walked into an auto salvage yard. It was there that a man, "Wild Bill," asked me the question that shook me — "If you died today, would you go to Heaven?" I could not say "Yes," so right then, I knew, it was time to give my heart back to God. I left there a renewed creation in Christ, my King. I found my joy and strength to get me through the days/weeks/months ahead.

After 25 years of living in Houston, Texas, where I had many friends and some family, I stepped out in faith, obeying God to move back to Mississippi to begin a new chapter. I will tell you I was scared because I really knew only my family and nobody else. Once here, I began networking with people and eventually was led to my church home. I now co-lead a life group for single women in my church along with leading our church's women's ministry. I talk with women who are struggling in their daily walk with God and in their home life as a single woman. I spend time with women who are broken in various ways to encourage them and help them to see that they are loved and that someone does care for them. It gives me such joy to see the transformation that takes place in those lives. I serve on the board for Teen Challenge of MS for Women, which is a faith-based rehab for drug and alcohol addicts. This is another place where I get to witness lives being transformed. I truly believe that God allows you to experience things for you to be able to help others.

My passion is helping people, especially those who are brokenhearted, hurting, or are elderly people needing help. God has given me a servant's heart, and I am called to serve where and how I can. In September 2020, I stepped out and began Hoop Cares, LLC. I'm using this business as a means to work with the elderly and their families to help them find resources to assist with their needs, to minister to women who have become broken and bruised, and to continue my online business, which promotes wellness utilizing all-natural products.

Today I am a firm believer in Christ and believe that we walk by faith not by sight. I pray and ask for guidance daily from my heavenly Father before making any decisions. He guides my footsteps all along the way. My greatest joy comes when I receive a message of thanks from someone whom I've talked to or worked with to let me know the impact it made on their life. I know that at the end of my life, the most important words I'll hear will be when I see my heavenly Father and He says, "Well done, good and faithful servant." (Matthew 25:21)

I've heard it said many times in the last several years, "God's not surprised by that". See, He knows the plan He has for us, and He knows what lies ahead of us. So, I've learned not to be surprised by the things that have happened to me — loss of job, Covid-19, temporary furloughs — He knew and prepared the way for me.

If there is something you feel you should be doing or have been called to do, then let me say this: DO IT, even if you must do it scared! If you feel ill-equipped, know that if God has called you to do something, He will give you the wisdom, the knowledge, and the necessary connections to those who can guide you.

Liz Hoop is an International Best Selling Author, speaker, communal leader, and tenured hospice community liaison. Professionalism, being the minimum standard in all she does, Liz attributes the cause of people; her greatest trademark. Having served many years at an executive level, in the areas of Marketing and Management; it has been a common thread of people-centric ethics that has ushered Liz into the vastness of philanthropy, overall.
Liz Hoop currently serves on board of directors for the Mental Health Association of South Mississippi, Special Needs Organization of South MS, Anchored Hearts Community Resources , Adopt A Grandparent Day and Teen Challenge for Women in MS; a complete echo of her heart's desire to serve humanity. She is also a great help within the local faith-based community, as Liz serves both; co-leader of a single women's life group and is also an appreciated leader of the women's ministry at The Springs in Hurley, Mississippi.

CHAPTER 9

A Tiny Seed of Faith

By Dr. Kathy Amos

"If you have faith as small as a mustard seed, you can say to the mulberry tree,
'Be uprooted and planted in the sea,' and it will obey you."
Luke 17:6

I can't tell you how many times the Holy Spirit has reminded me of this powerful scripture over the past 15 years of our marriage, when my husband and I by faith started our journey of building up the city where we currently reside. Although we were pastors who operated out of the gift of faith, there were many times that our faith was as small as a tiny mustard seed. We had no money, no assets, no wealth of wisdom, knowledge, or understanding of so many things that one would think should have been in place for us. We didn't even have a wealth of relationships. But we had love. We had faith even in times where it had dwindled down to the size of a tiny mustard seed.

I can remember when our three-year honeymoon had come to what felt like a squelching halt, and it was time for us to answer the clarion call of God to return home and build the city. He revealed His purpose and plans for what would be a 10-year journey of rekindling and building up of the faith of the folks in my hometown community in Canton, Miss., a small, rural city of about 12,232 people — the place where I was born and raised.

God has a mysterious way of raising up His children when we accept the call to rise up and be who we were predestined and ordained to be. He always does it with three key ingredients: faith, love, and obedience. Joe and I both came from broken marriages and a lifetime of broken dreams and visions — goals that were never achieved and ambitions that seemingly faded away with every passing year of our lives. But we got married knowing that God had a perfect plan of redemption and restoration, despite our past and our impoverished circumstances. His promise was the glue that bonded our marriage together when the days were so dark that even daytime seemed as dark as midnight. These dreary days were what caused us to fall even deeper and more passionately in love with one another. Although Joe was my bishop two years before our marriage, God didn't reveal to me that he was my husband until three months prior to getting married. We had a blended family of 15 children from previous marriages and relationships and four of our children remained in our care.

The beginning of our journey back to Canton started when we lost our beautiful 2,600-square-foot dream home in Madison, Miss. In our attempt to maintain a lifestyle that we started at the beginning of our marriage, we moved into another home just to find ourselves moving out after about five months. Thankfully, we met a couple, Don and Joanne Raymond, who had started a prayer group in Canton called "Pray Canton." This is where God opened our eyes of understanding to see His divine plan for the 10-year assignment called "Blessing Canton," the movement Joe and I eventually birthed.

We would have prayer gatherings and services at our small community church and in other places around Canton. I can remember holding services at our church, and no one ever knew that we were homeless and sleeping at the altar on an inflatable mattress every night. To be totally honest, those were the some of the best nights of our marriage. And yes, we even made love at the altar where we were married. We'd use our restrooms to clean up during the day; we'd go to work and remain faithful in carrying out the Father's business, despite our situation. One night after church service, a woman I had met from previous fellowships greeted us and began to make small talk. She asked, "Where are y'all living now?" We looked at each other, and I hesitantly said, "We're living here at the church and sleeping at this altar until God shows us where we need to go."

Voncele quickly replied, "No you're not! You're coming home with me until you can get on your feet." Voncele was our saving grace. We were able to continue doing the work of ministry in a bit of comfort. Our short stay with her gave us the strength we needed to continue pressing into His purpose and plans.

After a few months with Voncele, we moved into yet another home. Mind you, these homes were rental properties that we really couldn't afford, but we were willing to walk by faith to maintain that lifestyle of keeping up with the Joneses. I had landed a job in marketing at a local television station, but the job abruptly ended because of cutbacks and layoffs. I asked the Lord, "Now what? We're working hard and trying our level best to maintain what you've given us, and again it's been taken away!" God spoke to me in a still, small voice, "I've called you to full-time ministry to advance My kingdom. What I've put inside of you is far greater than any job you could ever have. You must walk by faith and not by sight." From that day to current, I've never worked another secular job.

The transitioning from place to place stirred up the gifts inside of us. With every move we made, God anointed us even more. Our prayer life went to another dimension, which ultimately activated the gift of faith in us. As we connected with our prayer partners and small church congregation, we began to gain momentum in the spirit and in the natural realm. We finally got some stability in a brand-new two-bedroom apartment where we spent the next eight years growing and developing in our faith. God began to open doors that gave us the opportunity to start community Bible studies and prayer groups. We even started a prayer group at Canton City Hall, where we'd go in at 7 a.m. and pray. Then we'd leave shortly before they opened for business. During those prayer times, God was anointing us to start the Blessing Canton Week City Transformation Revival. We also gained favor with our mayor, and I was blessed with my first assignment by former Mayor Fred Esco, Jr. and the city of Canton to be pageant director and coordinator over its first community-wide teen pageant, the Miss Hospitality Canton, Mississippi, Pageant. A few years later, I worked on a women's initiative with former Mayor Arnel Bolden. This is how the Empowering Progressive Women's Association was birthed, which transitioned five years later into a Business Empowered Mississippi Chamber of Commerce.

Our mission to start the Blessing Canton movement began with our bold tenacity to pitch a huge tent in the center of the Canton Courtyard Square and invite pastors, churches, community and business leaders out to revive our city. Keep in mind that we had no money, but we had a mustard seed of faith. Our first year hosting the event was a tremendous success. Mayor Bolden attended and played an active role in sponsoring and bringing The State of the City Address there annually. Each year we would take the love offerings of $2,000 and sow it into the city's budget to provide shelter and resources for struggling families. When the community read in the newspaper what we were doing, they began to partner with us. And every year God moved. He provided finances for the tent and the lunches that we served to feed the community. When we weren't in city revival, we'd gather the churches in the community and host an appreciation luncheon at City Hall for the city employees twice a year. This was our opportunity to fellowship, honor, and pray a priestly blessing over our mayor, aldermen, and city employees. We did this every year for 10 years.

God opened many doors for us during those years with our willingness to step out on that tiny mustard seed of faith. Today, I'm honored to say that we've come from sleeping on the church altar to being doctors in full-time ministry. We've founded and run a well-established statewide Christian Chamber of Commerce where I am the CEO. We own SOMA Coaching & Consulting, LLC, where we train, teach, coach, and consult with business and ministry leaders in professional and personal leadership development and event planning. Blessing Canton Week gained national recognition, and pastors in Jackson, Miss., started a similar effort called Blessing Jackson. We've received many awards and city proclamations from the city of Canton and notable and prominent leaders throughout the state and nationally.

I hope my story rekindles a fire in you and encourages you to live your faith out loud, even if you have only a mustard seed of faith. If God's word tells us that it's enough to speak to a mulberry bush and move it into the sea, surely, it's enough to build a city.

Dr. Kathy Amos is a dean's list doctor in ministry, a compassionate pastor, and servant leader, a nationally known empowerment speaker, a prolific trainer and teacher, and a results-driven multi-faceted coach. She's the founder/CEO of Business Empowered Mississippi Chamber of Commerce.

CHAPTER 10

Bus Trip to a Miracle

By Becky Mae Allen Farrell

It's one thing to say "I love Jesus." It's another thing to live faith out loud. Yet, here I am doing it! It has not always been that way. I was baptized Catholic, and my grandparents took me to church. But, at home there were fighting, hatred, non-belief, abuse, and loss — so much so that I left home at the tender age of 15.

Now, 15 is too young for anyone, much less a little girl, to take on adulthood. I searched for a safe place to land, and I longed for stability and love. I was fortunate to be taken in by my future husband's family. Yet, stability and love evaded me. For decades I lived believing that I was unworthy. I was filled with self-pity, blame, and shame. Life became something to survive, and my faith failed me.

Even though I was raised Catholic, bad behavior around me led me to make false and maladaptive ideas about God and myself. How I approached and responded to God was completely off the mark. I told myself that as a Christian, I could acceptably party, tell white lies, and skirt by in life as long as I went to confession, received communion, and attended church on holy days. This vicious cycle of faith is what I had most of my life. Regretfully, that's true even through motherhood.

As a single mother, I was exhausted all the time. Exhausted. Monday through Friday, exhausted. Saturday was even busier than during the week. I was so grateful for Sunday to come — finally a day of rest. We were very fortunate to have a church in our neighborhood with a heart for children's ministry. Every week, they sent a bus by for the children. Praise God that I had enough sense to get my kids on it. See, I loved God then just as much as I do now, but I was lost. I had a head full of knowledge, a belly full of false pride, and heart as hard as stone.

I was often convicted. Yet, I always fell short of the mark! Sure, I was smart. I was definitely an overachiever. Yet, I remained broken for decades. Like the man in John 5, paralyzed for 38 years, I was paralyzed for decades by my past failures and personal hurts. Yes, I was the first one in my family to graduate from high school. Yes, I graduated in the top of my law school class. Yes, my hard heart served me well as a litigator. Yes, I had a successful law firm. Yes, I kicked butt in the courtroom! But that darn mat (my past failures and false assumptions about God) tripped me up over and over and over and over again, UNTIL ONE DAY GOD'S LOVE BROKE THROUGH!

Well, you see, God used my sunshine soldier daughter who got on that church bus as a little girl to save me. Over the years, Britneye often invited me to church. I always declined. I was Catholic, after all. Still, she always invited. I always declined. Then, one day out of the blue, Britneye introduced me to Christian music. Boom, I was hooked! For the first time in my life, God's words washed over me and began to soften my hard heart.

I began listening to Christian radio and Christian CDs all the time. Miraculously, I began to learn who I really am. I began to learn whose I really am! I began to learn what amazing grace is and, most importantly, I learned who God is! Yesssssss! Yes! Yessssss! Lord, I want you! I want grace! I want love. I hear You! I have searched. All. Of. My. Life. For. YOU!

My faith slowly began to change, and my life reflected it. I was actually attending Christian concerts instead of rock concerts! Stop it! I know, I know — me, the ice princess at a Christian concert. And guess what else? I was saying kind things to people. I was even being nice to other lawyers. It was so strange at first.

I really loved how I felt at Christian concerts (now I know that I was feeling the Holy Spirit. But at the time? I was clueless!). So, I went to as many as I could because I wanted that feeling ALL. OF. THE. TIME. Today, I have that feeling (joy) most of the time because, at a concert six years ago, I got saved!

It was a sold-out Ron Meyers Production — Big Daddy Weave, We Are the Messengers, Lauren Daigle, and Jason Gray. I KNOW, RIGHT? How lucky was I?! Look, all I could get was ONE very last-minute cheap-seat ticket. And, I never went anywhere alone.

But this was BIG DADDY, and I loved "Redeemed." Sheesh, I was scared to death. The concert was a long way from home. It was dark. I was alone. Still, I felt like God really wanted me there. And, guess what? I was right!

HERE'S THE MIRACLE: I stood in line for hours. It was at a church, and it was super packed. They announced that I was going to have go into an overflow room for a screening (not live), because the live section was full. I was bummed. BUT GOD! Suddenly, a worker grabbed me, slapped a VIP bracelet on my wrist, and ushered me into the live section! She seated me in the center on the third row! WHATTTTTTT?????!!! It all happened so fast. My head was spinning. Like. What. Just. Happened?

I don't know. Just go with it, Becky. Just go with it. That night was amazing! The artists so connected with the audience! The room was on fire for the Lord. All of a sudden all of the artists wound up on stage all praying together over the room! Everyone in the room was praying! I was on fire! It was alive! I felt God breathing. I felt the Spirit of God! Many of us were. I then cried out to God like NEVER before. And the Holy Spirit filled me up with the love I longed for all of my life. I surrendered and I gave my heart to Christ! Instantly, He plucked my stony heart out of my chest. I felt it! He replaced that rock with a brand-new heart of flesh! I felt it! I WEPT! I WAS transformed by a Spirit! "A new heart also will I give you, and a new spirit will I put within you: and I will take away the stony heart out of your flesh, and I will give you a heart of flesh." Ezekiel 36:26 The altar call that night lasted for what seemed like hours. I don't know. I didn't want to leave. Many were saved. Many were healed. I was brand new.

I immediately joined a Bible-believing, life-giving church, took a Freedom Bible study, got baptized, and plugged into service and small groups at church! I attend church regularly and stay in my Bible. I pray and meditate. I pay it forward, for sure! Today, because of Christ, I live my faith out loud by ministering to children, women, people suffering from mental illness and addictions, and any soul whom God puts in my path. Because of Christ, generational curses in our family have been broken. Today, because of Christ, I live not as a woman of authority, but as a woman living under authority!

The best thing that I get to do is minister to children, just like God made sure that my children were ministered to. THAT IS THE MIRACLE! That is God's grace! It is the full circle! That is His unmerited favor!

God is certainly fond of the little children. According to His Word, "If anyone causes one of these little ones to stumble, it would be better for them to have a large millstone hung around their neck and to be drowned in the depths of the sea." Matthew 18:6. In fact, Matthew, Mark, and Luke recall exactly the same thing on the day that they tried to keep children away from Christ. Jesus exclaimed, "Hey, hey, hey — hold up. Suffer the little children to come unto me. Forbid them not: for such is the kingdom of God!" Matthew 19:14; Mark 10:14; Luke 18:16. In fact, Jesus was so empathetic that day, all three of them recall His saying the exact same thing — which kind of blows me away.

It is amazing to lead children to Christ! There really are no words to describe it. It is definitely supernatural. I recall each and every child whom God used me to save. But my greatest joy is when I am able to connect so profoundly with a child that God uses me train them to lead others to Christ. When I'm really lucky, I get a front-row seat and witness one of the kids use their new-found wisdom to lead another child to Christ!

Children's ministry is definitely my groove. I cannot thank God enough for allowing me the honor and privilege of repaying Him for bestowing His grace upon my daughter, who in turn led me and many of our family members to Christ Jesus! And to the unknown driver of the church bus, THANK YOU! Thank you, thank you!

Becky Mae Allen Farrell is founding attorney at the law office of Becky Farrell, PLLC. She has practiced law on the Mississippi Gulf Coast for 20 years. Becky is also an international best-selling author, speaker, and encourager, who uses her God-given talents to inspire women and minister to children.

CHAPTER 11

Allowing God to be the Author

By Serene Lee

The words we speak to one another have such an impact. I say this because I listened to the things people said about me. I listened to people tell me who they thought I was, what they thought I would become. I listened because, in some way, shape, or form, these people were people I loved or cared about. They were people who I thought loved or cared about me. Perception is a powerful thing. With words and perception, we can cancel someone's dreams. We can cancel their vision just by the words we speak. There are enough things going on in this world that are taking people out left and right. There are some being killed by the words someone speaks over their lives; this is a reality not spoken of. One would say ignore it or don't deal with those types of people. It sounds so easy; I have learned it is a mind-set. Renewing the mind is a real thing. Renewing my mind equals God's love, faith, life, and vision.

I understand the feelings of being pressed down and held back. I allowed others to dominate my thought process instead of remembering and claiming who God says I am. I was suffocating. My blood pressure was high; I would sleep for only three or four hours a night. I snapped at my family at the littlest things. I would sit in meetings, and my face would twitch as if I were having a stroke. I knew I was called to be a leader, but was this it? Now if I'm honest, in the beginning, the power excited me; it felt good. I thought this is what leadership looked like. While I was in a position of power, I was destroying people. My spirit became contaminated with doing the dirty work of others. The weight of this sent me into a downward spiral.

*My faith is what delivered me. It is my faith in the Lord
that I love to share with people because His joy is like no other.
He rescued me that day on my floor; He never left me.*

The darkness became a part of me, so much so, one day I was driving home from work after a hard day. I felt like the bottom was falling out of my career and my family. I felt I was not worthy, nor was I doing what I was called to do. I was so busy trying to be what people thought of me or live out the words that were spoken over my life, I forgot who God said I was. I was exhausted and over it all. As I approached the traffic light, it was turning red. The enemy whispered in my ear, "Just drive into traffic. Do this, and it will all go away." The whisper terrified me! I knew that wasn't God, and I knew it was not my thought. I wept the rest of the way. I knew in that moment I had to get home. I had to get to my safe place. I ran into my prayer space and wept. You know that hard cry where your face hurts, your eyes are burning from the tears, and you can taste the salt in them. That was on me on the floor.

The Lord told me, "You are functioning daily in depression." I wept some more. Me, depressed? I'm the strong one, I am the one who has it all together. It was in that moment I realized I was living other people's words and perceptions. The Lord asked me, "Do you want to be free, or do you want to stay captive to words and perceptions I never placed on you?"

After I got up from that floor, I looked in the mirror and wiped the tears from my face. It was in this moment I decided — no more. My faith started to stir up, and I began to crave more time with my Father again. I could no longer give the Lord mediocre prayer and worship. If I was going to come out of this, I had to be all in with Him, no holding back. I was going to be the leader God called me to be. I was not going to be defined by others anymore. I was not going to be a victim anymore by the perceptions of others. As a matter fact, I was going into the pits to help others get set free who are bound by words and perceptions of others. I was going to build and encourage those who feel stuck. Stuck is a mind-set, and there is a way out. His name is Jesus. He is a way maker and a burden bearer. He is the light to follow and will make the crooked places straight. In Him I live, move, and have my being. So, it doesn't matter what people have said about me or who they perceived me to be. The beautiful thing is, God is the author and finisher of my faith. He already wrote my narrative, and now I am going to speak it and write it. The key factor is, no one was there in the car with me that day; no one was there to pick me off the floor. As a matter of fact, my husband had no idea until after my encounter with God, and I told him.

I discovered leadership does not mean I need to be in the front or at the top. I am a conduit leader. I take the hopes, dreams, and visions of others and push them. That dark place was not for naught. It was training ground so I would know how to treat others and push them into destiny. I had to become bold, fierce, confident but still operate in a spirit of humility. There is difference between confidence and arrogance. That dark place taught me that, in spite of it all, I knew who my faith was in.

I live my faith out loud by encouraging others and leading by example the love of God. While I am not perfect, I strive to do things in excellence at the same time never forgetting others by demonstrating mercy, compassion, and grace. I know what it is to be a leader but not the head. I believe when we realize who we are, we can lead in the valley or on the mountain.

I had to really gain understanding of who I am and who I belong to. The promise is I'm refined. I didn't know about the process. The process is still equipping me and building me. My faith is what delivered me. It is my faith in the Lord that I love to share with people because His joy is like no other. He rescued me that day on my floor; He never left me.

Serene Dumas Lee is a wife and mother. She is currently enrolled in Liberty University where she is a doctoral candidate in strategic leadership. She is the founder and CEO of Rhema Women's Center where she coaches women in leadership, goal setting, performance and spiritual formation using Biblical principles. She is also the founder and director of Rhema Institute of Leadership, which offers online courses for professional development.

CHAPTER 12

God's Peace in the Eye of a Storm

By Dr. Sheila E. Sapp

My business partner and I were excited and looking forward to what was ahead as co-owners of an educational consulting business. We had just co-presented at our first National Youth At-Risk Conference in Savannah, Ga., at the Hyatt Regency on March 10, 2020. This was our third year as a consulting business, and we hoped to see the fruits of our long hours of research, planning, and designing. We were certain lead contacts would materialize after the conclusion of our presentation. Our session was well-attended, and the session evaluation feedback responses were positive and affirming. We knew our participation in this conference would open new doors and additional opportunities for us.

I must admit that I had become apprehensive about going to Savannah as a presenter. My daughter called several times insisting that I cancel and go another time. She stated that several large organizations had canceled or rescheduled their conferences because of the Coronavirus. I began to get nervous and decided to contact the university sponsoring the event to see if they were going to have the conference as scheduled. There was no change. So, I prayed and asked for God's protection and took several bottles of hand sanitizers, made sure I washed my hands, refrained from shaking hands, and stayed clear of anyone coughing. I bolstered my uneasy feeling by telling myself that God made this possible. Our presentation proposal was selected to be presented along with many others. The week following our presentation at the conference, schools, colleges, and universities were shut down in the state of Georgia, as were schools in other states. The country came to a standstill. Our consulting business and elation over the prospect of really soaring as a business was short lived.

What were we going to do now? What would this shut down do to our new business? No school, business, college, or university would be contacting us for assistance. I was thankful, however, that I arrived back home safely, but I spent days washing my hands numerous times during the day. Nights consisted of lying in my bed wide awake, unable to sleep, wondering if I had been infected. How could something like this happen in our country? I was living in fear, doubt, disappointment, and uncertainty.

I felt like I was in a storm with no place to go to escape the devastating effects of the Coronavirus. One morning, as I stood before the bathroom sink washing my hands, I winced after applying hand sanitizer. Looking down at my hands, I was shocked to see how the constant washing and applying hand sanitizer had given them a dry, withered appearance. I could not continue living like this. I did not leave the house for two weeks after the statewide shutdown. So, I decided to start walking around in my yard to clear my head. While I was walking, a movement in a nearby tree caught my eye. I turned and saw a gray, bushy tailed squirrel. I followed the flight of the squirrel up the tree and found myself looking up at the sky. I was overwhelmed with the beauty of the white, fluffy clouds on the backdrop of the clear, blue sky. I was filled with a sense of peace and calmness. Suddenly, I knew I had to move from my current state of mind. I needed to continue to pray and seek joy and encouragement. To help look for joy and encouragement, I stopped listening to the radio, watching the news, and reading articles about the coronavirus. I began to spend more time reading my Bible, participating in online Bible studies, and online workout sessions. I began walking daily in our local, small park. I felt God's presence even more as I walked, prayed, and talked to Him. I was filled with such a sense of peace, that I began posting positive words on my Facebook page to encourage others who may have felt like I did.

Being relatively new to Facebook, I spent time learning how to do simple tasks such as uploading photos, videos, sharing, making posts public, screen-shotting posts, and creating content using software applications that were new to me. Eventually, as the pandemic continued, our co-owned consulting business was terminated. We decided to pursue our own separate passions. This decision, however, enabled me to spend more time on my own personal consulting business, Sheila E. Cares Educational Consulting and Services, which was suffering from neglect, lack of focus, and attention. It was time for me to strike out on my own and walk a different path. My desire to encourage, share, empower, and connect with others opened a new journey for me. I wanted to tell and share what I did to gain a sense of peace during the coronavirus storm that had impacted many lives.

I spent hours watching YouTube tutorials and questioning others who were more skilled and adept with social media. I had to overcome my fear of making videos or going live on Facebook. My self-consciousness made me tongue-tied and unsure of what I was going to say. I began to doubt my abilities. Additionally, fixating on being perfect and not making mistakes led to procrastination and a lack of confidence.

Trying to be perfect was an unrealistic and limiting expectation I put on myself. One day during a walk in the park, I asked God to help me conquer my fears. My lips were trembling, and my stomach was fluttering as I got on Facebook and selected "live" after my prayer that day. I did it despite fear! I was on for only a few minutes, but I survived. When I finished, I was shouting praises and thanking God. I have been doing "lives" and videos ever since that day in the park. I have also participated in several podcast shows, sharing my story, vision, and passion with others.

To share how I obtained peace and a sense of calm during the pandemic, I decided to broaden my audience by reaching out to other women needing encouragement to help them cope emotionally during this storm. Since I am in the at-risk category for the coronavirus, I could not have in-person sessions.

I opened a Zoom account and learned how to use it. As a result, Sheila's Chats became a reality. I use the chat time to encourage, check in on people, and have discussions on different Biblical principles. Currently, my group is small. I am now using this time to strengthen my spiritual and Christian walk to serve.

"And let the peace of God rule in your hearts, to which also ye are called in one body; and be ye thankful."

I have always been a believer of Christ. Now, however, I am deepening my relationship with Him. I call and rely on His presence, strength, and guidance daily. I keep an "I am grateful" notebook in which to write what I am grateful for every day. This helps to keep me grounded and appreciative of what God has done in my life.

I know I am making an impact by the many positive comments I receive from my postings, such as "Thank you, Sheila, I needed to read your posting today." It warms my heart and encourages me to keep striving to expand my business and seek God's direction for next steps.

I would strongly encourage anyone who has a dream or a desire to serve others to take that first step after praying and asking for God's guidance and direction. Sometimes we have our own expectations of what will happen and when it should happen without seeking God's will.

Remember, each of us has different skills, talents, and abilities. We are unique and endowed with specific tools God wants us to use to serve Him. After many years as an educator and school administrator, I am now fulfilling some of the dreams and desires of my heart. I have had to enter the world of social media, which was foreign to me. I am still learning and not limiting or blocking myself with demands of perfection. Whatever your dream, desire, or goal is, you already have the necessary tools required. Someone is waiting for that program or service you have in mind. Act now. God is waiting to walk the path with you. He will hold your hand throughout your journey.

Dr. Sheila E. Sapp is a retired educator and former school administrator with years of experience serving parents, students, teachers, and school leaders. She is the founder and owner of Sheila E. Cares Educational Consulting and Services, LLC. Using her faith, expertise, and educational background, Sheila encourages others to walk in their purpose and utilize God-given gifts and talents. Dr. Sapp resides in Woodbine, Ga.

CHAPTER 13

Champion of Faith

By Tamekia Green-Judge

Anear-death experience caused by a rare diseases would likely have taken me out if I had no faith. I was not a champion of faith at the beginning of this. I went through a period of several surgeries and bouts of depression, fear, and anxiety, not knowing whether I would live or die. By the end, faith was all I had. I stood on the foundation of a God that was faithful and limitless. With His grace and healing, He performed a miracle.

The doctors said that I would not live, but God said that I shall live and not die. With the performing of a miracle, faith was manifested in a manner like never seen before. Faith helped me to see with a different perspective, to see that I would live and not die, that I did not have to believe the negative words of the doctors, as they spoke death. I now had the ability to speak life to myself, as I believed in a God that was true to His word.

I held on to God telling me that this disease would not take me out. Never did I imagine that I was kept for a purpose of ministering to those who came across my path, no matter where I was. Once I was healed, people would come up to me and started telling me about what they were faced with. Who would have known that it would be issues where healing was involved?

I was now being used to encourage people and remind them of who God is: Jehovah Rophe, the healer, the healer from the inside out — restoration to make us whole. My purpose is to encourage, to reinforce the spiritual eyesight versus the natural.

A lady came into my office one day, and I could sense that something was wrong. I asked, "Are you okay?"

She responded, "I just received some bad news from my doctor, that I would not be able to have kids."

I looked in her eyes and said to her, "I was told the same thing, but I know a God that said differently."

This was yet another health issue that I was faced with, when man said I was not going to be able to have children, but God said differently. When I had my son, my faith was increased to another level. It seems like lately, no matter where I am, there is always someone who enters my presence, and I am able to ignite the faith within them.

One of the most famous stories in the Bible, the one of David defeating Goliath, is the ultimate underdog story. The story has become synonymous with a less-favored opponent beating a favored one, as in David beating Goliath. What was a giant opponent in my life turned out to be a miracle because of faith. What giant opponent is in your life?

A pure heart allows God to accomplish any good work through anyone. Is your heart pure? If not, you must work to make it pure by following the commands of the Lord. You should not fear the unknown and should trust the living God to help you move in faith as I did. Saved by grace and healed by faith.

Tamekia Green-Judge graduated in 1998 from the Technical College of the Lowcountry, Beaufort, South Carolina, with an associate's degree in general business. She obtained a certificate in small business management along with a certificate in education. Tamekia continued her education at Park University, Parkville, Mo., in 2001, where she obtained a bachelor's degree in management. In 2004, Tamekia earned a master's degree in business administration.

Tamekia and her husband, James, started Cam Cam Enterprise, LLC, a long-haul trucking company. Tamekia is also a seasonal tax professional.

Tamekia and James L. Judge reside in Dale, S.C. They have a 14-year-old son, Cameron.

CHAPTER 14

A Lasting Spiritual Growth

By Dr. Josephine Harris

As a military spouse, I have experienced and seen different aspects of various cultures and met people from diverse backgrounds. We all learn from people with different backgrounds. As a military spouse, I learned to adapt to different environments and the culture I endured (military community). I remember when we were stationed in South Korea. I was working on my research study by attending the graduate program at Walden University. I received an email from my school stating, "We have a mission trip to Negril, Jamaica, coming in August of 2019." I never dreamed of going on a mission trip with a university. I thought churches and other worshiping organizations mostly did it. I was filled with joy and excitement. Then, I wondered how I would fund this trip. We had just relocated. How would I cope with another new environment? Would I miss this fantastic opportunity because of lack of funding, or not go because I was afraid of another culture shock? Then, I began to pray and pray about the self-doubt and financing.

I talked to my husband about this mission trip and explained the self-doubt and my concern about the cost of this trip. Keep in mind that we had just relocated to South Korea. I was still worrying about the funds, but God made a way. After filing our relocation paperwork (due to a permanent change of station to South Korea, we received additional funds that were due to us. Therefore, I was able to pay for the entire trip in full (look at God)! As stated in Matthew 7:7, "Ask and it shall be given you; seek, and ye shall find; knock, and it shall be opened unto you."

After arriving in Negril, Jamaica, the group and I checked into the lodge. I was tired and anxious, so we all went to our rooms to rest so that we could be well-rested for the next day. The next day, the group and I went to Negril Elementary School and delivered school supplies and items that the school needed. Seeing poverty firsthand affects you in some way. I saw school-aged children who didn't have school supplies or even shoes. I helped in a crowded classroom with no working air conditioner, only small, desktop fans. After we gave the principal and the assistant principal some school supplies, books, clothing, and shoes, the smiles and looks on children's faces were unforgettable. The joy of the children, teachers, and officials was also remarkable. The faith and strength they had were incredible!

After my mission trip ended, I was faced with new experiences and discovered new depths to my faith. I made a small but lasting impact on the Negril Elementary School that we had served. And while the trip may have been over, the good news is that I had the opportunities to grow and help others, such as I did in South Korea. I taught English to Koreans (both children and adults), also provided therapeutic services through an International Counseling Center in Seoul.

As an international licensed therapist, I am moving forward to make even more mission trips.

Sometimes, we like to think that preachers and missionaries are the only individuals called to fulfill the work of the Great Commission, but in fact, we are all expected to bear witness to the saving power of Jesus Christ in our lives, regardless of whether we went to seminary or theology school.

Participating in a mission is to grow in Christ, and the experience allows us to grow in our faith as much as it allows us to serve others. Whether you can go on a mission trip or not, I am challenging you to start living like Jesus. Volunteer your time, donate, or even just quit complaining, and you will notice how much happier your life will be. Going on a mission trip is remarkable, but living with a missionary heart in the real world is phenomenal.

For over 13 years, Dr. Josephine Harris worked as a psychotherapist with extensive cases of clients with mental health and developmental disabilities from various backgrounds. She operates a coaching/advocating and consulting business and is an author and the CEO/founder of Calming Minds, LLC, a positioning and coaching firm that helps consultants and inspires, and encourages others who connect with the mind, body, and soul as they relate to mental health and healthy relationships. Dr. Harris is a wife and mother of seven children. She has nine grandchildren. She is a military spouse, empowerment life coach and domestic violence/sexual assault advocate, as well as an entrepreneur. Through her Healthy Minds & Hearts blog, she enjoys encouraging others through transformational message of professional and/or personal growth using inspiration, facilitation, coaching, and other dynamic mechanisms that allow her to encourage, motivate, and empower women of all cultures.

CHAPTER 15

Trust Leads to Triumph

By Errin C. Baugh

I spent the first 20 years of my career working in corporate America. I was tested and tried over and over again over the span of my career. During this time, I got married, gave birth to two children, received the Lord as my Lord and Savior, went back to college, and graduated from college with two degrees. From a performance perspective, I received several promotions and bonuses; life was good. I was riding the wave of good success and God's favor, but it did not come without faith challenges.

What I failed to mention is that I worked for the same company for 20 years and in the same office. My professional footprint was indelibly made in this office. I started my career as a background investigator and ended my career as the city manager. A lot happened between 1988 and 2008, but for the purposes of this assignment, I will fast forward to years 2006-2008.

In February 2006, my life would be forever changed. I was presented with an opportunity to serve as the interim general manager for our office because the former GM was moving on to greener pastures. I was tapped to lead the office, and I along with others saw this as a natural progression, considering I was number two on the leadership chain for our office. I was excited and ready and for the next six months, I was on a mission to show the executive leadership team that I was the right choice. Our office finances increased; employee morale improved; raises and bonuses were earned and given; personal accolades were given to me by the CEO and our group VP during this time, so naturally this position was mine.

In July 2006, I received a call that shattered my expectation of leading this office as general manager. The leadership team chose another person to become GM and placed me back in my role as number two in the city manager's position. The news came with a vague and almost scripted explanation. I allowed the shock to come, but I realized that I had to quickly speak with my team before the grapevine gave them the news. Fast forward, 24 hours later, I was on my planned vacation with my family, hundreds of miles away, to be with my thoughts, my feelings, and to plan my next move. From front row, seat 1, to front row, seat 2.

My faith was shaken. I was faced with how to demonstrate the leadership that I had often talked about; now I had to walk it out in front of my employees. I had to walk the talk, and this required me to be transparent, authentic, and to live my faith in God out loud, demonstrating courage and leadership in the face of disappointment. Initially, I was not okay. I felt angry, disappointed, blind-sided, embarrassed, relieved, anxious, and let down. I felt like I checked all the boxes, excelled in the areas that made us profitable, and yet it was not good enough. Even during this time, I could sense the hand of God on my life, so although my ego wanted to leave, I did not at that time get the green light from the man upstairs to go, but He was sending me signs. This time period reminded of the scripture in Proverbs 19:21, "There are many plans in a man's heart; nevertheless, the Lord's counsel that will stand." We all have plans and desires, but they must align with the will of God for our lives. This was a door that the Lord closed: Hear me good–the Lord closed this door because He had a greater calling for me.

In February 2008, another shift came, a closed door, the end of an era. I celebrated 20 years of service in February 2008. We had an office celebration; I received a company gift and the promise of more years to come. Seven months later, in September 2008, I found myself one Monday morning in a conversation with the GM and the HR director, and I was informed that, as a result of company re-engineering, my services were no longer needed. I received a folder filled with separation papers and what was stated to be a fair and equitable severance package. Within 15 minutes, I was back in my SUV, driving home. From celebration to separation within seven months. In the spiritual realm, the number seven is the number of completeness and perfection. God clearly showed me that it was time for me to go. My assignment in that place was complete. The end of an era.

Where was I going? What would I do next? Leaving a place that was so familiar to me was one of the scariest things that I had ever had to face. I was leaving the place where I had basically grown up as a young adult, as a young career professional -- a place where I had invested my time, talent, creativity, and energy, and it was no longer open to me. God closed this door never to open it again. This also happened at a pivotal time in our family life when we were preparing our son for college. He had just entered his senior year in high school, and there were so many expenses, but at the forefront of my mind was college and how my current situation would influence or affect our financial commitment to his collegiate journey. Can you say, "But God?" But God had a plan.

In August 2008 (one month before my separation), my son and a few of his classmates were called into a meeting to discuss a scholarship opportunity through the POSSE Foundation. His counselor and teacher encouraged him to apply immediately as the deadline was looming. He applied and was asked to come to the first round of interviews, which happened to be on the same day that I was terminated from my job. Did you hear me? Yes, on the same day that I was released from a 20-year career, my son went to his first POSSE scholarship interview. From separation to an appointment with destiny on the same day. The POSSE process has three interview levels before the scholarship award announcement is made. God took my son through all three interview levels and awarded him a four-year tuition scholarship to the

College of Wooster. The scholarship was valued at over $100,000. Did you hear me?

Philippians 4:19 reads, "My God will liberally supply your every need according to his riches in glory in Christ Jesus." Not only did He move for my son, God said, "I have your son, and I have you as well."

Within 75 days of my separation, God placed me on assignment in the city of Atlanta. He put me in this place at a lower position and lower salary. Humbled. Selah. He opened the door for next while I was working through my now moment. Starting in this new place was my now — lower position and a 25-percent pay cut. I was so anxious that I cringed about accepting this assignment, primarily about the salary. "How am I going to do this at this salary?" questioning God. I was thinking of my bills; I was thinking about changing careers at 40 years of age. I felt a lot of anxiety over this change. I need to add that I am a tither and have been for a long time. Tithers can call on God to do for them, because they have been faithful stewards.

On my way to next, our God, who does not need our help today, tomorrow, or anytime in the future, was leading me to a place of faith and trust in my finances at a level at which I did not imagine that I could trust God. I was moving from a place of familiarity and trust in my own doing to a place of leaning on and trusting in God. "Lean in" took on a whole new meaning; I was in the midst of leaning on the arm of God while leaning in on the goodness of God.

> *"Count it all joy when you fall into various trials, knowing that the testing of your faith produces patience, but let patience have its perfect work, that you may be perfect and complete, lacking nothing."*
> — James 1: 2-4

God was also showing me that when we are found to be trustworthy and faithful over the least, He will make us ruler over much. Over the span of my first six years in this new place, my God gave me a $60,000 increase, which far exceeded the salary of my former place of employment. Twelve years later can I tell you that God is still doing His good work in my life on this assignment? He has favored me and promoted me into my next.

Eighteen months ago, He increased me again; He found me again faithful and added to my leadership mantle. In the span of 12 years, God has doubled my former salary, and for good measure He added 25 percent. I just want to remind everyone that God has the last say-so in our lives. When we think that we can't, God says He can. From angst to confidence in God.

I am living my faith out loud by sharing my story to empower others to get into the driver's seat of their lives. I do it through serving others in my family, the marketplace, community, and my local church. Living my faith out loud has not come without challenges, but the rewards have been greater.

Errin Baugh is the Deputy Chief Information Officer in the Department of Atlanta Information Management leading the Enterprise Project Management Office and the Business and Fiscal Administration Office. She is also the chief executive officer of Leading Like A Girl, LLC. Errin is the author of "Get in The Driver's Seat: Taking Control of your Life and Career." She is a Certified Leadership and Life Coach and has also co-developed a life coaching certification training program. She formerly served as executive director for the My Sister's Keeper Foundation for Women, focused on moving women from average to excellent. She serves on the board of directors for MSK Foundation for Women and Grace Church International. She is an adjunct professor at Georgia Piedmont Technical College and a licensed minister at Grace Church International. She holds three degrees including a master of arts in leadership, bachelor of science in organizational leadership, and associate of science in business. She has attained several professional certifications. Errin lives in Conyers, Ga., and has two children and two granddaughters.

CHAPTER 16

UnWanted - UnSpoken

By Lisa G. Dunn

The pool, warm and welcoming, received me
Embraced, secured me
Although premature, you seemed to assure
We'd endure
I see you
Empty handed, but full, so carrying and burying me
Foolishly, it seemed in an Unspoken place
Grace filled me deep in your tortured space,
Rocked me to sleep in your rhythmic waist
We were there, Together...
I opened your womb door without knocking
Mistook heart gaping gates for a welcome mat
I barged in, not welcomed
Unwanted
Shock popped passion's fantasy with reality
Girlfriend's whispers slice this twice
Mistake, serial error confirmed in cold, sterile offices
My presence, affirmed
Tears and dread called me, Unwanted
Embryonic silence
Cells multiplying, compelled this
Divine reality enveloping
Loose leaf letters...
She wrote an Unspoken story
Resignation, reluctant acceptance
She embraced me,
Lied and denied
I was Unwanted

I was 14 years old attending Mrs. Reed's home economics class at Hayward Junior High School. It was my favorite class. Freshly baked cookies, made from scratch, cupcakes and some simple meals ushered us to a class full of excitement and engagement. This was one of the few classes that allowed us to socialize while we learned. The subtle, "I'm preparing you to be a good wife and mother" message rose and was entangled in the asbestos way above our heads. Oblivious, we just loved our paired-up jabberwocky, eating and seeing the pictures from the cookbook on our plates. Giddy moments our teenage mouths adored, most of the time.

Trauma often met us in our sanctum, behind Mrs. Reed's back. Once I poured out my rage onto the slick Formica. I claimed to hate a spoiled younger sister who most teens at the table saw as flawless. My home life, chaotic at that moment, was well-to-do by most standards. My suffering had nothing to do with basic needs, but was a burning knowing, like fire in a dream. I seemed to chase smoke and mirrors. This day, I don't know the cause of my tearful release; all I remember saying is, "Dad always takes her side. He doesn't even act like he loves me. I don't think he's my dad!"

We were five children in a city of secrets,
but none of my siblings knew "the Unspoken."

A hush enveloped the table. Our collective shock caused a silence that made Mrs. Reed give us that church mother look that takes your breath away. Everyone turned the page in their cookbook while I wiped my tears. When teaching resumed, someone asked me if I was serious. I resumed my tirade with a long list of the special things he did for her and not for me. Then, I repeated, "I don't think he is my father!" This was over 40 years ago, and the unexpected response still seems scary-movie ominous. My friend's eyes seemed to giggle from across the table when she said it: "He's not."

No one knows that my heart stopped. These girls who shared my life, daily, did not know that my head almost hit the floor. Not one person noticed that blood had stopped flowing to my brain. The lump in my throat was invisible to them, but that sentence was choking the life out of me. So, breathlessly, I lied and said emphatically, "I know!" My soul communed with the asbestos ceiling, now a safe place to escape a reality my young mind was unable to process. My entire life shattered on the blue and white fake marble pattern. I played with globs of gum as she chewed me up in front of our friends.

Most teenagers hold the unspokens like eggs made to be broken, secrets made to be told. Of course, she easily cracked me wide open. Her syllables chiseled away at my truth. She destroyed the illusion my mother worked so hard to hide like flames attacking butter. My unwanted secret scrambled with giggles while spoons sampled today's buffet. Before the bell dismissed us, I knew his name, his kids' names, his wife's name, and like sparks from my nightmare, a fire smoldered in my gut. When the bell rang, everyone scattered.

I grew up in a middle-class African-American neighborhood. My parents, like most, purchased land and built us a new home. We were five children in a city of secrets, but none of my siblings knew "the Unspoken." My mother married, and my older brother and I were adopted by the only father we knew. Dad was powerful and passionate. He said what he meant and dedicated himself to family and community. We enjoyed family vacations, bowling, athletics, and church. We were always engaged in some emotional tug of war, but I tired of losing, so I just shut up. The Unspoken never emerged in our discussions, like adoption papers brought him a curtain of amnesia. He just didn't care. The Unwanted almost totally destroyed my relationship with very loving and supportive parents.

My mother lived ashamed. Her secrets, hot coals in her soul, forced her to speak the unspoken for moments before she passed away. She died before I ever explored the deep wounds in my soul caused by years of unanswered questions and feeling unwanted. She died before all of my unspoken questions were answered.

In 2020, during the COVID-19 crisis, I found Shannon Evette's Sanctuary Ministry. I realized I had never addressed the resentment and shame-based lifestyle I was conditioned to live. The solitude gave me time to examine my soul's bruises and scars. I asked God to keep me safe as I opened the gates of my wounded psyche and let Him in to do His perfect work. I gave the Holy Spirit permission to correct and challenge my thoughts, habits, and the stories I told myself. I rejected the need to pull back and distrust people. I walked my little girl through grief and loss issues. I asked God to restore her name and her faith in her purpose. Most importantly, I forgave others and myself for exacerbating my childhood wounds. This gift of healing renewed my passion to write, speak, and help others transform their journal entries into beautiful poetry. The Word says that He will give us beauty for ashes. Let the journey begin!

God peeled back my shame and spoke His Truth
That hush that happened when I entered His divine space
Around the throne, pre-me, heavenly seated, called to be…
I was wanted, maybe needed, their eyes pleased me
Open and airy, high and exalted
They wanted me there
They welcomed me where smiles miles wide saw me
Hugs pulled me into all that was glorious, clean, and pure
Each with sameness of joy, different expressions
Impressions upon, into and through me
Triune in tune, they moved me,
My Father, love, power, His is heartbeat
My Brother and Savior, love, sacrifice, in touch, is lyric
My Spirit, love and wisdom in whisper's breeze, is melody
And my soul sought harmony, swayed engulfed,
We embraced music
Safe in unity, divine oneness,
They call me Song
Singing an anthem of destiny, purpose
Sweet release, free flow
In the fullness of joy, I agreed, to go
Immediately, from there, I was conceived

I eased into newness, consuming passion
Earnestly, historic giggles welcomed intimacy,
All my glory became their sad secret, still I was lyric
All freedom became confinement, I was heartbeat
We were becoming one, separately, I was melody
Oh, so close, but distant
Me and She played hide and seek, but He did not find or speak
We made a secret, Unspoken

Who's this Her as close to me as They were
They, distant now, as I sleep in this restless place
Her sleepless showcase, spotlight hot with shame and pain
I heard my name, Song again
And increased Their volume to drown the Not Wanted noise
Her abhorrent, bitter and deadly blues going through me, at me
I sang Her my song loud, but Her trauma drowned it out
Still I sang…sang an unwanted song to my unwanted self
Forming in an unwelcoming place…

I searched for Them in a reckless gestation, air-tight embrace
Absent from this body were they
But deep in my soul Their pieces of my song sang
I heard hope for me
Then finally, after an unseen eternity, captivity delivered me
Destiny turned my face and pulled me through a passageway
From prison cell called womb
Into a new camp, colder than the heavenlies
Sterile and damp
Someone examined and cleaned my new heaviness
Wrapped my members and delivered me to Her breasts
She washed her cheeks with joy's overflow
I heard Her hope song, it echoed mine
She called me Lisa Gail, Oath of God and God rejoices
She didn't know They called me Song, but it's OK
Today Her eyes surrendered to my being
My here posed less threat, just a heavy dread
Draped in her shame and contradictions
Unspoken, but God's Oath proclaimed
Unwanted, but God rejoices
Strange contradictions working
Together, as we sing and strive to
Commune in harmony
Joyfully, meekly exchanging
Ashes for beauty

Lisa G. Dunn, aka Soul X Sighted, from Springfield, Ohio, transforms life's challenges into rhythmic words, rhymes, and faith-filled stories. Champion for the underserved, Lisa thrives when supporting children, teens, and the disenfranchised, pointing the way to draw beauty from the ashes of their lives.

CHAPTER 17

Mission Accomplished

By Timothy Johnson

One New Man. This is the name I gave to the ministry that has taken me outside the walls of the church. It speaks to the nature of transformation through Jesus Christ. It is the focal point of Ephesians 2, specifically verses 14-16, which says when the temporal and fleshly things cease to bear importance, we can allow the purpose of Christ to manifest in the earth through us.

In the spring of 2015, One New Man was established as a 501(c)3 that presented itself as a band. We began gigging as a worship band, "charging" attendees non-perishable products, feminine toiletries, canned goods — all to donate to domestic abuse facilities, soup kitchens, and human trafficking recovery centers. The ministry was phenomenal. Worshiping among racially diverse, varying denominations, while covering various worship songs, choruses, and hymns, this ministry thrived. We toured Southern Baptist, Pentecostal, and United Methodist churches just to name a few. We toured multiple states, including Ohio, Virginia, Louisiana, Texas, and more, seeing God not only provide for the needs of the organizations we set out to support, but also make a difference in the lives of the people involved.

Having grown up in church as a musician and then as a worship leader, I knew the effect true worship could have on people. As a sort of "secret mission" underneath the known mission, I wanted the Lord to use One New Man for unification. In the midst of true worship, surrendering all that you are to Christ, unveiling the sins that we attempt to cover, God can change you from the inside out. When you completely disrobe the heart and allow Him to impregnate you through the Spirit, that "thing" that you need will be birthed in your life! Can you imagine a room full of people fully pouring out their hearts before the Lord? All of them in one accord? Sounds like a headache for the kingdom of darkness, right? Most definitely! I know in my heart of hearts that this could be the kind of people who, just like in Acts, were said to have turned the world upside down. Ever since I was a child, I had dreamed of being a part of something so transformative.

At the age of 6, I remember attending church at Bethel Assembly in Pascagoula, Miss. I don't know how we began going there, but I do know they had an elementary school back in those days, and my parents sent me there. Maybe that's how it happened that we started attending. One Sunday as service began, there was no drummer. And no matter how hard everyone tried, they just couldn't catch the rhythm of the song they were trying to sing. Without being asked, I went onto the platform and started to play the drums, giving them the rhythm they needed. It was in that moment, the moment of God's people singing together and attempting to enter the presence of God, that I knew I always wanted to be a part of this. It's here that I'll point out that being a child brought a necessary simplicity to this idea. Jesus compared the kingdom of Heaven to a child along with the faith of a child being deemed a good thing. And I truly believe that worship of the true and living God is best done with a childlike heart, knowing that Daddy loves them no matter what and wants to be in their presence as much as they long to be in His!

As life went on, there would be many experiences that would make me question the heart — the heart of God's children who would enter church buildings across the country Sunday after Sunday and leave without any indication that they'd been to the throne of the Most High and where they'd live week after week in a weakened state, seemingly run over by the devil, with no appearance of grace in their lives. Understanding that I'm not perfect in any regard, I had only two options: search or ignore. Search out the reasons why some allowed themselves to live outside of the victory the word of God that was theirs, or ignore the issue altogether and just do me. Well, I lazily searched ... the scriptures, at least. I began to recognize that many of the people in the Bible who all-out worshiped the Lord in depth were those who were in the midst of great trials and recognized that God was the only one who could deliver them, or it was those who had been through something terrible that the Lord had delivered them from, and they were worshiping Him for it.

So, I thought to myself, "Maybe this is why people don't worship passionately. Maybe they don't need Him for more than salvation. Maybe the worship for that is done in their lives, and they're simply waiting to arrive in heaven after death occurs, and they'll pick up on their praise. Perhaps everything in their world is fine, and they attribute that to God, and the praise for this continual circumstance is past." I honestly had no idea. I couldn't imagine that either theory was true. But in the midst of it all, the goodness of God in my life kept swelling up in my heart. I had survived poverty, homelessness, and abuse in the ministry by so-called believers, many of whom had fallen away at this point, but experienced the Lord's continual provision in situations that looked hopeless. And I began to write a song ... "All my praise to King Jehovah, He is good..."

As the worship flowed in my heart, I had to "put it on wax." It was not a matter of believing that anyone wanted to hear it, but a matter of remembering it, because so much would pour from my heart so fervently that I couldn't contain it. People who were close to me would ask me to come to their church and share what had been born out of my personal worship. And I did. It was an amazing experience to be living my faith out loud in the presence of people who not only longed for but connected to the raw intensity of my expression of worship before the Lord — the kind that didn't care what I admitted, as long as I didn't harbor a secret sin; the kind that was louder or was faster in tempo than their denomination allowed.

It was after this that I knew what I had to do. It was the door the Lord had opened to help me fulfill a desire that I'd expressed many years before. I would live my faith out loud by holding concerts for the express purpose of multi-cultural, multi-racial, and multi-denominational worship where we would ask the Lord to reveal how to be a blessing to others in need outside the church and maintain a unification in the Spirit. One accord. No one would be there who didn't want to be there, because this wasn't a church service. There was no offering unless you decided you believed in the ministry going forth and you wanted to be a part of that ministry financially. I named the effort One New Man. The oneness in Christ, exemplified by the first church in the Bible, would be the earmark of this ministry. A newness in purpose and authenticity would be its foundation. Mankind helping, healing, representing the second Adam, Christ our Lord, would display the passion that accompanied our worship!

To date, we have traveled to multiple states and helped multiple organizations across the U.S. We've ministered in and supported multiple denominations and their in-house charitable ministries; been a part of many other musical venues that have shown a light on what our ministry was doing for the Lord; delivered countless boxes of clothes, food, and other items to local food banks and women's centers. God has received the glory and the honor. Holding live events has been impossible to do in light of recent world events, but the music of the heart of worship will continue to flow!

Timothy P. Johnson is a husband and father to four beautiful daughters. He enjoys living Christ out loud, playing music, cycling, and skating. He works part-time as an engineer, producer, musician, and in various other capacities within the music entertainment world. Timothy is thought well of by most everyone who really knows him, and he aspires to be a blessing to all he encounters.

CHAPTER 18

As Though Working for the Lord

By Ken Tims

Growing up a middle child in a family with nine kids in Minnesota, I learned a lot about living my faith and serving others at home. Besides taking care of us kids and teaching piano lessons, my mom always had an extra plate of food for the hungry folks who showed up frequently at our back door. My mom made every person she met feel like they were her favorite. Needless to say, her funeral was packed.

My dad was a hard-working grain salesman who regularly shared his salvation testimony with his customers. Although not always popular, Dad broke sales records and actually replaced all the other salesmen in his company. It was apparent to me that God's favor was over our family.

The two of them brought us to church whenever the doors were open, and on Sunday afternoons, we visited the nursing home, where Mom played the piano and each of us kids played an instrument. But at age 20, I was drafted into the Navy, where I was exposed to some worldly pleasures that I'd never experienced before. Don't get me wrong, I was not perfect even when I was in my parents' home.

All of us kids had paper routes or other chores to do to contribute to the family budget. But I always held on to a few dollars to spend at the local pool hall. I liked to have a good time even then. But overseas I was captivated by the exotic sights, sounds, and adventures to be had in foreign countries and had an active social life that included a lot of drinking and partying.

One year I lived in Nairobi, Kenya, with a Danish friend who introduced me to some of the "finer things of life" enjoyed by members of the diplomatic community overseas. My Christian upbringing kept me from going overboard, but I found myself stretching the limits my parents had set in some areas. After about a year in the military, I found myself in Guam in a worship service in a church called Melody Chapel, where people were obviously enjoying the presence of God. Instead of crying, which is what people did in church at home, these people were smiling and happy, freely raising their voices and hands.

This experience touched me deeply and stirred a desire in me for something more — a closer, more intimate relationship with the Lord. During my eight years in the Navy doing construction work as a Seabee, I saw a lot of the world (over 25 countries), met some good friends (including my future wife, in Moscow, of all places), and had some exciting adventures while

Many of the inmates come from homes without a father to love and lead them. I try to affirm them and communicate God's unconditional love for them. Some former inmates are now program instructors. The chaplain feels we are making a positive impact and has made a video of the classes, which he shares at churches. I know I always leave the jail with a spring in my step, knowing I've brought some encouragement to some men who need a smile and some life-giving words. I have also noticed that some of the inmates who receive the Lord and begin to apply the truths of scripture are actually more free and happy than many walking around on the outside caught in drug addiction and other bondage, ignorant of the good news of Jesus.

working for a State Department unit that performed maintenance on secure areas of American embassies around the world. Although I made some effort to serve the Lord during this time, these were mostly just religious in nature. I continued to send my tithe to my home church, seek out and attend church services where I was stationed, and I enjoyed helping local missionaries procure supplies. I helped one missionary in Japan procure typewriters and another in Nairobi, Kenya, get door locks for a Bible school.

But after a while, the double life of fun-loving Ken and Christ-follower Ken was becoming a strain. So, in October 1980, even when the government offered me a position I had thought I wanted, in Beijing, China, I turned it down and resigned from the Navy. Although my first plan was to return home to Minnesota after leaving the service, I decided to go to Gulfport, Miss., instead. (I was home-based out of Gulfport in the Seabees and started attending a church there between deployments.) The pastor of this church happened to call me and offer me room and board in his home in return for construction work on a new church building. During the year I lived with Pastor Rowe, I got right with the Lord, went to community college to earn a degree, and wrote letters to Cathy, the girl I left behind in Moscow. At the end of that year, Cathy and I married in the church we had both attended in Washington, D.C., and then moved together to Gulfport. We both served in several areas in the church in those early days and are still serving there today.

I first attended this church in 1973 when it was called Grace Temple upon the invitation of a friend in the Seabees who heard about it in Guam. When the pastor of Grace Temple, Pastor Rowe, felt he should go to a different area of town and build a larger building, he renamed it Northwood Christian Center.

Over the years many people have come and gone, and many changes have taken place, but I have never felt a release from the Lord to leave. Once when my pastor was preaching out of Ezekiel Chapter 37 about the dry bones, he called me out and said, "Sometimes the Lord will take the bones of a man from Minnesota and plant them in Mississippi." I guess that is why I have remained planted in the same church now for 47 years. Over the years, I've helped build five church buildings (Northwood has added three more campuses) led worship (only when there was no one else to do it), taught Sunday

School, led small groups, was an usher, a greeter, an elder, and a serve group leader. Some of my serve teams were quite large, since God gave me favor with other men and women who liked to work and serve the Lord with gladness. We cleaned up yards, built ramps for handicapped people (at least 50), and did minor home repairs to roofs, fences, etc. Those who received our help knew we cared about them and were not there for money or other personal gain. It brought us all a lot of joy and fulfillment to be the hands and feet of Jesus.

I also went on several overseas missions trips sponsored by our church — to Mexico, Guatemala, Nicaragua, Honduras, and Russia. These usually involved some type of construction but also gave me the opportunity to share the Gospel and my own salvation story. My most recent mission trip involved helping run baseball camps for youth and adults in Cuba, where we were able to share the Gospel. Seeing people receive the Lord as Savior was always the most exciting part of mission projects.

Since retiring after 25 years of working in the Contracts Department of the Navy, at Ingalls Shipbuilding, I enjoy teaching classes at the Adult Detention Center of the Harrison County Jail. The class is called Authentic Manhood. Many of the inmates come from homes without a father to love and lead them. I try to affirm them and communicate God's unconditional love for them. Some former inmates are now program instructors. The chaplain feels we are making a positive impact and has made a video of the classes, which he shares at churches. I always leave the jail with a spring in my step, knowing I've brought encouragement, faith, and hope to some men who desperately need to hear the redemptive love of Christ. I have noticed that some of the inmates who receive the Lord and begin to apply the truths of scripture are actually more free and happy than many walking around on the outside caught in drug addiction and other bondage, ignorant of the good news of Jesus.

I also care for a 93-year-old lady who does not receive help from her family. I was not able to be there for my mom and dad during their last years, but believe the Lord put her in my life to help her during her last years. Although she lives in a personal care home that provides her with meals and basic needs, I act as her power of attorney and help her pay bills and maintain communications with her family. Although she can be a bit cantankerous, I know that God has been patient with me, so I persevere in helping her.

Colossians 3:23 says, "Work willingly at whatever you do, as though you were working for the Lord rather than for people. Remember that the Lord will give you an inheritance as your reward, and that the Master you are serving is Christ." I have written here a lot about what I have done for the Lord. But He has done much more for me. My good health, happy marriage, wonderful kids and grandkids, friends, house, cars, money in the bank — these are all blessings from the Lord for which I am grateful. His Spirit in me, leading me and guiding me, comforting me in times of trouble, and correcting me when I go off course has made all the difference, and I know that in the life to come it will be even better. As my dad often said near the end of his life, "The best is yet to come."

Ken Tims retired from the Naval Reserves (Seabees) and from the Department of Defense, Navy, SUPSHIP Pascagoula. He has lived in Gulfport with his wife, Cathy, for the past 40 years. The two have three children and nine grandchildren. They are both enjoying life and attend and serve at Northwood Church in Gulfport.

CHAPTER 19

The Power of Words

By Jaime Norwood

Mississippi heat in the middle of September, sixth-grade anxiety, and girls on a bus with no air conditioning — this was the perfect environment for what should have been a forgettable argument, except this would be my first encounter with words that take actual root in my life. While riding the bus home from school, one of my neighbors and I got into a heated argument, about what I have no idea. As we got off the bus, the argument continued to our front lawns. From the corner of my eye, I could see her mother watching us intently. I don't know what I said to provoke that lady to say what she said next, but what I do know is that her words haunted me for years afterward. She began screaming at me like I was the neighborhood stray dog. I think she said every cuss word in the book. But when she said, "That's why you gonna end up pregnant before you turn 16!" Everything in me was shaken. What would possess her to say such a thing? What's worse is for the next few months she made it her life's mission to spread ugly lies about me. Words, especially false ones, have this way of taking flight and creating a life of their own. I was so hurt by the things that were said that I just wanted to hide away in a hole.

Although those words were untrue, there was a secret I kept locked away from everyone. This secret gave those words so much power in my young life. At the tender age of three, my life was turned upside down by the boy from next door. Unwanted kisses, touching, and exposure was what I endured until the age of ten when the family moved away. I wish I could tell you that he was the only one, and when he left my abuse ended, but that would not be the truth. There were so many men touching me that I felt as though I had a target on my back. And what made it worse were the things that women said to me. I was always called "fast" or "hot in the tail." Whenever people saw me, especially older women, all they could see was sex. I guess in some ways, what they were discerning was correct. However, the part they missed was how sex was happening to me. What they weren't aware of was that I was being mishandled by grown men.

I didn't know the effect that words could have on a person, but I later discovered just how powerful they are, especially as I began to watch the words come to pass in my life. See, my neighbor's mother didn't understand the power she possessed. She didn't know that the power to speak life or death lied within her tongue (Proverbs 18:21). And when I found myself pregnant at the age of 17, all I could think about was the day she said those words to me. I realized at that moment, her words had taken root in my life, and I was desperate to find a way to stop living under the curses that had been spoken over me. I cried out to God for help! I grew up in church, so I had always heard about Him, and I believed He was real. I just hadn't experienced Him for myself. I thought my life was over, but what I didn't' know was that God was about to take me on journey that would set the course for the rest of my life.

The next few months would go on to be one of the darkest times of my life. Five days after giving birth to my son, we found out that he had a rare heart condition that would require him to undergo triple bypass heart surgery at just two weeks old. I was in a failing marriage that eventually ended, and I felt like my world was spinning out of control. After several months of living in the hospital, Kaedon was well enough to come home. A good friend of mine invited me as a guest to her church. With so much going on in my life, I was desperate for a change, so I went. While I was there, an announcement was made about a weekend-long event called The Encounter that the church was hosting. Something in me knew I needed to be there, so without hesitation I signed up.

As the week of the event approached, I began having doubts about going. It required so much work to take care of Kaedon, and I didn't want him to be a burden for someone else. I made up my mind that I would stay home, and I lay down to take a nap. While sleeping, I had a dream that was so disturbing it caused me to jump out of my bed and rush to the church. I don't have the time to share the full details of the dream, but I can tell you this: In the dream I saw the coming of the Lord! It felt so real. I woke up shaking and crying. I knew that I had to get to this encounter event, and encounter Him was exactly what I did.

That weekend I learned about spiritual warfare, soul ties, word curses, and so much more. I learned that I needed to come out of agreement with the negative things spoken over me and come into agreement with what the word of God says about me. I learned that God has a purpose and a plan for me, and the enemy will stop at nothing to throw me off that path. I learned how to wage war with the enemy by applying God's word over my life in every situation I faced. God's word is the most powerful weapon we can use against our adversary, and when it is coupled with prayer, the enemy doesn't stand a chance! "For the weapons of our warfare are not carnal but mighty in God for pulling down strongholds, casting down arguments and every high thing that exalts itself against the knowledge of God, bringing every thought into captivity to the obedience of Christ." (2 Corinthians 10:4-5) All my life the enemy used negative words to entrap me and keep me in chains, but God was beginning to teach me that His word had the ability to dismantle all the lies of the enemy!

The more I studied God's word the more my faith grew. God was showing me that the life I always dreamed of having was at the tip of my tongue. All I had to do was speak it! I knew that I had to change my language toward myself. I began searching the Bible for scriptures about rejection, healing, fear, self-esteem, love, and joy and prayed them out loud over myself. I wanted to find biblical truths to combat the lies that I had spoken over myself and that others had spoken over me. As I did this, I noticed that the way I thought about myself was changing. I was becoming mentally and emotionally stronger. The word of God was literally changing me from the inside out, and I'm here to tell you that He can and will do the same for you!

I know many of you reading this may be living under the shadows of what your mother or your father spoke over you. You may even be facing hardships due to the negative words that you've spoken over yourself. I'm here to tell you that you can change your life right now by declaring God's word over yourself daily! Today I am the wife of an amazing husband and mother of three beautiful boys who love and adore me even after I was told that I was hard to love. I have a master's degree in social work even after being told I was slow and wouldn't make it through college. I am a homeowner, business owner, and I have an amazing career in social work even after being told that I would never be good for more than lying on my back.

As a school social worker, I have the opportunity to live out my faith every day by mentoring young girls and boys and encouraging them to be all God has called them to be. I have the amazing opportunity to be the one who speaks words of affirmation over them. I teach them to speak positivity and blessings for themselves and others. I also have the amazing opportunity to live out my faith through my local church, serving in leadership and sharing my testimony with the body of Christ. I believe that I am living the life I live today because I refused to believe the lies of the enemy and began to declare God's word over my life. Brothers and sisters, I implore you today to fight back! Use God's word to disassemble the lies of Satan. Fight for your future! Fight for your marriage! Fight for your children! Fight for your health! Fight for your peace! Whoever said sticks and stones may break my bones, but words will never hurt me was lying! Words will kill you, if you don't learn to take authority over them and replace them with words that bring life.

Jaime Norwood is a native of Gulfport, Mississippi. She is the co-owner of The Chop Shop Beauty and Barber, a worship leader, and a licensed social worker. She obtained her master's degree in social work from The University of Southern Mississippi. As a counselor and speaker, she strives to propel individuals into their God-ordained destinies.

CHAPTER 20

Growing Long Faith

By Von M. Griggs-Laws

Perhaps, just as I do, you have a lot of stories about big moments and single events that alter the course of your life. I don't believe faith can be summed up in a single chapter of a person's life or a single event. For me, the single events and circumstances over time have caused my now faith to increase. My faith today resembles nothing as it did in 1972, when I first made a confession of faith publicly at the age of 12 years old. I followed tradition as expected while attending New Bethlehem Baptist Church in St. Louis, Mo. The age of 12 was the significance of children being like Jesus acceptingly; it was the age of understanding. Without full understanding, you made a confession of faith, repented of sins, and invited Jesus into your heart. And so I did. There was no way of my knowing then that that would not be a one-time, done-it-all event that was to cover the rest of life's occurrences. Rather, it was my entry to faith. I have repeated that process thousands of times on this journey.

A middle child of five children, I was often mocked by my siblings for seemingly having more faith in what or who I couldn't see. Each month, I walked two blocks from our home to the Open Door Outreach ministry to get my pocket-sized book to read. I would sit in my bedroom window and read it, though not always understanding. Sometimes the words gave me a comfort that was unexplainable, and yet it was a practice of habit that would increase my faith through very hard, lonely times. I've learned that transformation in Christ is a lifelong process, not a one-time event.

As a result, the little miracles we string together to form our faith stories don't always hang in a perfectly straight line; there are dips and twists and even tangles. My testimony is a collection of the little miracles God has performed throughout my life, some personal and others observed from watching God work in other's people lives, even when I had the audacity to think they didn't deserve God's blessings.

My growing faith has allowed me to trust God when He did not answer my prayers and hopes. It was painful, but necessary, to surrender to God's sovereignty and believe His decisions for my life were made out of His love for me. Faith showed me the necessity to not compare my life with others. As a divorced single mother of two children on active duty in the U.S. Air Force, My faith was shaken with the embarrassment of a failed marriage and not making promotion alongside my peers.

Trusting God continued to grow over time, which increased my faith.

While others would tell me to just have faith or say that my faith was not strong enough, I really was not trying to prove to anyone that I had some supernaturally-developed faith muscles.

I continued to read books on faith and inspiration and hope in conjunction with several versions of the Bible. That habit led me to faithfully knowing God had greater plans for me, and how He wanted me to serve His people. In 1998, I accepted my ministry ordination, and I would have highs and lows of this calling. As an intercessor, I've learned the tenacious faith that comes through worship and warfare. I remember reflecting on the angels who had watched over me and my children during separations, and how I had escaped death after being at gunpoint on three occasions. Those reflections caused me to accept God's call on my life. Faith that He would do just what He said.

I grew to accept the faith of the Proverbs 31 woman (I did not always feel that way) because she appeared so perfect. However, as my children were growing older, I could better relate to her. That unnamed woman had what I consider to be long faith. I consider she looked into a distance, beyond where her family's situation was. She had learned of God and could trust Him to provide for her family. Like her, I read the promises of God and increased my faith to move beyond what was happening at the moment and look further into what He says will happen. And when prayers are not answered the way I think they should be, I have faith to know that whatever the situation is, it will turn out for my good.

"She looketh well to the ways of her household, and eateth not the bread of idleness".
Proverbs 31:27

If you were to break this scripture down using the Hebrew definition of the words "looketh," "well," and "way," it would read more as this: In an effort to discern better, she leans into seeing at a distance the steps of her family members. Believing God, her faith was increased as she looked forward to God's provision. It had not happened yet, per se… yet her faith told her it would. This is what I mean by having long faith. I believe this is the stance we must all take as we continue to believe in God's word and the witnesses He has called us to be. Long faith is ultimately necessary for our jobs, in our communities, our governments, etc. We don't see all that God has, yet He promised it would be a good, finished work.

Due to many circumstances, I have had to exercise my faith, and my faith muscles have become stronger over the years. My greatest accomplishment, and the way that I live my faith out loud, is to share my honest, personal stories with women going through transitions in their lives. I live my faith out loud by working with women going through changes, inspiring them to fight through anxiety and fear to gain clarity with faith, purpose, and power for joy on the journey. Perhaps a woman is fearful of moving forward (job loss, unexpected career change, divorce, death of a loved one, etc.). She's anxious about starting over, discouraged, or embarrassed by the change in life she is facing. I live my faith out loud by listening first, helping them determine where they want to be, what resources they currently have to get there, and what resources they will need -- all on their own terms. I encourage them to wake up old dreams and desires, create new outcomes, embrace where they are, and determine the next steps, to create a gratitude journal and celebrate along the way, discipline the disappointments and keep it moving with joy.

In living my faith out loud, I offer personal, private coaching services and provide leadership training for women in first-time supervisor/manager positions.

My prayer for you is that your faith will be increased and that you waver not at the promises of God, that you live in peace, and have a hopeful and joyful future. Dear reader, keep hope and faith alive.

Von M. Griggs-Laws is an author, coach, cleric, and CEO and founder of Griggs Safety Consultants, LLC., and Joy Restored Outreach, LLC -- two specialties by which Von is both an inspirational and highly-sought-after trainer, coach, and advocate, practicing occupational health and safety and advocacy for homeless female veterans. Her chosen vocations have afforded her the opportunities to speak to many audiences. Her most celebrated talks have been The Essentials of Safety & Health/ Preserving Life & Limb, Your Joy Can Be Restored, and You Are Not What Happened to You. Von is also a well decorated communal leader, retired U.S. Air Force veteran, and ordained minister. She has accumulated several honors, medals, and awards for her unyielding commitment to excellence through philanthropic efforts. When she is not out serving others, she is a proud wife to her husband, Maurice Laws, a blended parent to ten adult children, and a loving grandparent of five.

CHAPTER 21

Just Like Daddy

By Pastor DeBo'rah Drayton-Ward

My painkiller of choice was hating. As a little girl I was forced into the clutching arms of anger, insecurity, depression, bargaining, loss, and grief. In 48 years, I have never been accepting of why I had to grow up without a daddy. Why did all the other kids have a daddy, but I was not able to have one?

From the book of Exodus in the Bible until today, there are still present-day pharaohs in the lives of the people of God. Some of our pharaohs are behind our suppressed, shut doors and are resurrected daily when we press the rewind button of the past. Some of our pharaohs are triggered visitors through our feelings of regrets, on the streets of our neighborhoods, and in our workplaces. What is the name of your unthinkable pain? How long has it been hurting you or you ignoring it? I would like to share with you my ex-anguish and grief.

I lost my daddy to police violence because of a mistaken identity. He was wearing his long, black minister's robe, going door-to-door sharing the Word of God with people. I have been told he did this regularly in the streets and neighborhoods of Detroit. The plainclothes police officers were looking for an adolescent black man who had just robbed a liquor store in the neighborhood. The suspect was wearing a long, black coat.

It was explained to me that when the three white officers, who were not in uniform, located my daddy, they ran and charged behind him with drawn weapons as he was walking. Witnesses say they called him "nigger" and told him to stop. Possibly, my daddy had no idea who they were, and he did not stop. They killed him, and when one of the police officers turned my daddy's body over, he said, "Oh, it's a nigger preacher," (probably concluded by my daddy's robe with the crosses on the front). The same officer also stated, "We got the wrong one." The second officer present replied, "It's just another nigger," and they walked away. My daddy was killed a couple of streets over from my grandmother's house where I was playing outside.

In life, you will experience trauma that will catapult you from being at the top of the world to the world being on top of you. My husband lost his job for reporting racism spoken toward him. My daughter could not visit certain school classmates or friends because of an open expression of racism. I did not permit my son to purchase his dream car because of my fear of racial profiling. As recently as a year ago, I experienced verbal racism at my former job; after reporting it, I received two calls, and the case was closed.

When the presence of the Lord visited me, He made known His sovereign ultimatum: my choice to live in hate would prohibit me from the blessedness and my birthright of the Kingdom of God. Regardless of the catalysts-law-breakers who caused extreme devastation or traumatic events that caused destruction, whether it is a criminal past, addiction, health issues, sexual assault, dysfunctional or a broken family, immorality, death of a loved one or political turmoil – I was taught and learned to hate, which tormented me. However, it was always my choice to decide the harvest of sin or a harvest for my soul.

By faith, I tell myself as the big girl instead of the little Deborah, "You will miss feeling like a daddy's girl, his one and only, his favorite, and you did not get to make that choice. Deborah Jean, I speak to those things that plague you, to rejection, severe traumas, and every single pain inflicted on you, the spirit of vulnerability and your desire for protection. You have buried this pain deep and long enough in trying to hide it and protect yourself, both present self and the child your once were. I see you. I hear you. I feel you. Accept your healing through the mercies, the love, and the bloodshed of Christ. Take and give love by faith. Live your faith out loud without ceasing, even when you do not understand why. Deborah Jean, as hard as you can, exude faith when you're not feeling it. Allow your daddy's love to be resurrected in you as Christ was resurrected by His Father's love. Receive Christ's strength-building courage in testing and the beauty of God's amazing grace to inspire others when you're not helped. Do your best, Deborah Jean, to live your faith that shows the only way you know how. You are performing for an audience of one – Father God."

I asked my family, friends, and co-workers if I live my faith out loud and how? I am told I live my faith out loud by being real, true, and faithful. In everyday life I show compassion, take time to actively listen, and/or offer practical solutions, and share hope on the personal matters. Talking and walking the walk and showing others it is not simply something you talk about; it is being an example of the Father's actual love. In vulnerable times with sincerity, I demonstrate my beliefs in good times and bad times. Despite personal tragedies and adversities, I will and have preached the gospel to an empty room as God leads me.

People are impacted by our hearts of passion to care for people in every walk of life. Living faith out loud involves helping others to see themselves better, not bitter, and walking into victory. It is important that Christ's love shine through us so brightly that people are drawn to Him. Living faith out loud is the inspiration that causes people to strive to be better, to become that voice of justice. Compassion is essential toward one another, regardless of skin color. Jesus is always the answer to our problems, and we must share Him out loud for the sufferers in silence and the misguided.

My daddy lived his faith out loud until the day of his death. When my daddy ceased to exist in my life, my Father God was there. My experiences, my pain, and being comforted by the Comforter are why I can live my faith out loud. I live out loud for my daddy in Christ who has been there the entire time.

DeBo'rah Drayton-Ward is a pastor of Women of Wisdom Ministry and King Shepherd Ministries. She is a recognized prophetic voice, teacher, third-generation preacher, conference speaker, senior tax analyst, finance coach, and tax presenter for schools, businesses, and social groups. She writes "Pull Up", a daily encouragement on Facebook. She is intricately involved in marketplace ministry and is community servant-leader and volunteer. Her father was an Air Force veteran. She has been married 39 years to her husband, Eric, an Army veteran who serves with DeBo'rah in ministry. They have two children and three grandchildren.

CHAPTER 22

Living, Laughing, Loving Loud With a Purpose

By Robin Killeen

A ll of my childhood, I was told that I was LOUD. I talked loud; I sang loud, and I laughed loud. I was constantly shushed and told to use my inside voice. I was asked questions like, "Do you have to sing that loud?" "Can you tone it down a little?" "Can you try and whisper when you talk?" I was labeled as loud, which created an intimidation within me, a spirit of rejection.

I tried really hard not to be me; I became an imitator based on the crowd that I was in. I guess you could say I was a learned chameleon, a people-pleaser, non-authentic, and I performed to be accepted. I remember agonizing over simply wanting to fit in; I just wanted to be normal.

Fast-forward to adulthood, I enjoyed a 24-year successful career as a young female manager in the staffing industry, where I continued perfecting my performance skills as a people-pleaser. Upon my promotion to regional manager, I purchased a navy-colored business suit along with a new pair of eyeglasses that I did not need to assist me to see. I felt I needed the glasses to look smarter, more mature, and worthy of the role of a regional manager.

One day I was meeting with a large prospective "client", and he stopped me in the middle of my presentation and asked me, are you okay? He proceeded with his next question, "Are you seeing things clearly?"

I thought these were strange questions, but I answered, "No, I see fine; why do you ask?"

He said, "One of your lenses in your glasses is missing." My heart was pounding, and thoughts were racing through my mind that I just might be exposed as a fake. I kept my composure and calmly thanked him for letting me know, then finished my presentation. The good news is, thankfully, I did get the contract. You see, because of the labels spoken over me as a child, I had learned how to excel at being non-authentic, a people-pleaser, and a performer.

Even with all my professional successes, I was discontent and felt as though something was missing. I began to search for the components missing from my life. One day, I had an authentic encounter with God and found out exactly what had been missing from the equation. I made a decision to re-dedicate my life to God. As my mindset began to shift, I no longer wanted to perform to be accepted. I wanted to be the real me that He had in mind when He formed me in my mother's womb. I learned that He called me by my name and that I fit in perfectly with Him. He told me He designed me to be unique and that I could be my authentic self, loud and proud.

Through God's unfailing love, He helped me understand that the power of His love is not based on performance, position, abilities, nor the decibel level of my voice. What? I cannot believe what I am hearing! What a relief! What freedom! Thus, living in Him, I can live out loud! He was canceling all the labels that had been spoken over me and that I bought into.

God was transitioning me from a performance position to my purpose. All this time, He was grooming me to step into the fullness of His purpose and calling on my life. In 1999, He entrusted me to start a marketplace ministry called WOW, Women of Wisdom Inc., where we empower and encourage women of all ages and backgrounds. We encourage each other to live and love out loud. Now, I didn't answer this call quickly; it took some convincing on His part that I was ready and capable. The road toward God's purpose for our lives will not always be lined with roses. However, looking back, I'm able to see the blessings in those times of the excruciating growing pains.

What label has been put on you and is holding you back from living your life out loud? What has been said about you that you bought into? More im-

I was asked questions like, "Do you have to sing that loud?" "Can you tone it down a little?" "Can you try and whisper when you talk?" I was labeled as loud, which created an intimidation within me, a spirit of rejection. I tried really hard not to be me; I became an imitator based on the crowd that I was in.

portantly, who does God say you are? What does God say about you? When you start to view yourself through God's eyes, you gain confidence and can truly start walking in His purpose for your life. We are made in the image of God. You are a beautiful creation and a reflection of Him. You are a masterpiece! Jeremiah 1:5 says, "Before I formed you in the womb, I knew you; before you were born, I set you apart!"

The key to living life out loud (LOL) with purpose, is in knowing the ONE TRUE God! When we spend time and get to know Him on a much deeper and intimate level, we understand all that He has given us to live life both successfully and out loud!

Now that I have discovered the greatest of truths, at last I know who I am and whose I am. He continues to teach me how to live out loud, laugh out loud, and most importantly love out loud. We can do many things in life, but the only thing that remains is love!

My goal in this life is to be authentic, transparent, leave a permanent mark, and a Legacy of Love (LOL).

1 John 4:7 says, "Dear Friends, let us love one another, for true love comes from GOD."

Robin Killeen, founder of WOW - Women of Wisdom, Inc., established in 1999. WOW is a non-profit marketplace ministry that encourages and empowers women from all ages and all walks of life. Robin is retired from a 24-year career as a regional manager for a multi-staffing firm. She currently invests in real estate/flipping houses. She is past president of the Biloxi Bay Chamber of Commerce. She has been a member of the Jackson County Chamber of Commerce for over 10 years, serving as board member, chairperson for the ambassador committee, and chairperson for Leadership Jackson County. A member of Lighthouse BPW Business & Professional Women for over 15 years, Robin has been ambassador chairperson for Mississippi Gulf Coast Chamber of Commerce for 10 years and has served on the board of directors. She has served on the Praise team at Cedar Lake Christian Assembly for over 15 years. She is a member of Unified Coast Prayer Movement. Robin is the recipient of the Sam Walton Award from the Mississippi Gulf Coast Chamber of Commerce, Woman of the Year award from Juniper Tree organization, and the Lucimarian Roberts Humanitarian Award. In 2019 she was recognized by Success Women's conference as a Mississippi Gulf Coast Top Influencer and in October 2019 received recognition for 20 years of public service from Gov. Phil Bryant's office. In 2020 she received a proclamation from the city of Gulfport naming February 17 Robin Killeen Day. She was most recently the recipient of the 2020 Forever Young award by Coast Young Professionals and The Mississippi Gulf Coast Chamber of Commerce. Robin resides in Biloxi with her husband, Pat Killeen. She has two children and five grandchildren.

CHAPTER 23

Faith is Personal — but Never Private

By Dr. LaTracey McDonald

I remember packing up my house and being told by God that the mountains that I had created in the form of boxes were not going with me. This faith journey was personal but never private. I was transplanted from Minnesota to Mississippi eleven years ago and shown the promises of God in such a miraculous way during a pandemic; it was an understatement to faith in action.

I heard the voice of God when I received the promises and confirmation of owning a full-time publishing company, having three daughters, being full-time in ministry, that my husband would find me here, and the three-bedroom house. Did you believe that this process was done with confidence and ease? Of course not! Faith makes things possible, not necessarily easy, to say the least. To live my faith out loud meant that I had to walk this thing out even when I didn't feel like it, sometimes alone, when the pain from silence was ever present, when church wasn't the safe haven I was raised for it to be, nor when my gifts didn't open the doors I expected, I yet had faith.

I was expecting a harvest as soon as I showed up in Mississippi because I was obedient, right? A delay is not a denial, they say. I did my part, so why did God allow this to happen to little old me? His servant! Preacher! Teacher! Daughter! I knew that I had sown seeds and my expectations were high. Blessings on blessings were happening, but not the ones I thought. I believed God was going to supply every one of my needs, and yet, what was taking him so long? I had a harvest to reap!

I know I am not the only one who hesitates in life when God instructs us to do something. Partial disobedience is still disobedience; I have found that to be true. What was the benefit of doing what God told me to do, if I would have to silently endure certain circumstances that caused pain and suffering because the church was no longer the safe haven I was taught it to be?

Without faith, it is impossible to please Him, for whoever comes to God must believe God exists and that He rewards those who seek Him. (Hebrews 11:6)

I did that, I thought! I fasted and prayed! Only to be in Mississippi with two daughters waiting on what God told me would come to pass. I was waiting on the reliable testimony. Let me try this another way.

Hebrews 11:5-6 says it's impossible to please God apart from faith. And why? Because anyone who wants to approach God must believe both that He

I was expecting a harvest as soon as I showed up in Mississippi because I was obedient, right. A delay is not a denial they say. I did my part, so why did God allow this to happen to little old me. His servant! Preacher! Teacher! Daughter! I knew that I had sown seeds and my expectations were high. Blessings on blessings were happening, but not the ones I thought. I believed God was going to supply every one of my needs, and yet, what was taking him so long? I had a harvest to reap!

exists and that He cares enough to respond to those who seek Him. I can be honest and say that my faith wavered often, and yet God remained faithful.

It's accurate to say that the promises of God were true, even in my disobedience. Who am I to ever doubt Him? I remember when God told me to move and not to take the materialistic items with me to Mississippi. Only for God to prove Himself over and over again.

The house I was shown in my dream was a three-bedroom house, near the water, on stilts, and while I saw the signs that said, "For Rent," I was led only to contact Mrs. Carpenter (notice her name), and she asked me to come to her home as she had just broken her leg. Oddly enough, I blindly went to her home to tell her what God said about this house in my dream. She asked me specifically how much money I had at the time — with only a day left before I was scheduled to return back to Minnesota. I told her that I only had $150. She stated the application fee was $50 and that I would need about $25 to eat. The remaining balance of $75 would be my rent amount, because God said this was the house that was for me, and she also believed.

I left the cars in Minnesota! Yes, you read correctly! Multiple cars were left there, because God said so. Only to arrive here in Ocean Springs searching for a dealership that would lease a car to me as a business owner new to the area. God sent a woman by the name of Mary (notice her name as well), to deliver a free vehicle to me, with the title and keys, exactly like the one I had just seen at the dealership.

As for the husband, I thought I could assist God with this one, 'cause you know He needs our help sometimes. Laughing at myself, I sit back and think of all the times I thought God really needed my help, especially when I was trying to rush His timing in relationships. I went out and "found" a few prospects I thought would fit the promise of God, only to learn that a good idea isn't necessarily a God idea. So, I find myself whole and single in 2021, still waiting on God, because His word is true and, if He has fulfilled EVERYTHING else, why would he leave this one unfulfilled?

Never in my wildest dreams would I think that the promise of giving birth to purpose would be naturally as well as spiritually. So, to hear the doctors tell me that I had cervical cancer and that I'd never give birth again, my faith wavered tremendously though I still had to minister to others in the midst of my pain.

Write Your Way To Healing is not only one of my signature programs, but the way God used my writing to heal me and make me a vessel to assist others in the process of their publishing and writing.

While I was healing from cervical cancer, God told me that I was birthing purpose. Remember, God promised me to be full-time in publishing? So, I (not God) prematurely started Purposeful Publishing and Consulting only to have my life's experiences be exposed. Over time, all lessons became blessings, and the greatest need that I had as a black author was birthing, not only a new business, but also the global movement, Black Authors Rock.

Do you think I would have been obedient and moved to Mississippi if I had known that I would be without my family and friends while recovering from cervical cancer? But God! You read correctly, I recovered fully, and, even while I tried to cover up my sin, God still blessed me with a healthy baby girl who is 8 years old today. The birth of everyone's purpose is truly a household name and not just a promise fulfilled.

Life naturally has four seasons, but the way global warming is showing out these days, things just aren't as normal as we've always known them to be. It's not what they called me; it's how I answered. Since I moved to Mississippi, it was a struggle for those in some of the local churches to acknowledge me as a minister. I was frustrated and disappointed that I could work in the church, and yet my gifts weren't recognized. I know that titles weren't the focus, and yet not having the proper spiritual covering after living here for seven years impeded my growth. In the spring of 2017, God decided to bloom me where I was planted in ministry. God had called me to nations, and after I decided to become licensed and ordained, God opened doors for me here in Mississippi and internationally.

Over the years, I have always seemed to live my faith out loud! The faith-walker, as I am affectionately called, has shown me that as bold as my hair color is and as unapologetically black as I am, as I walk out my God-given talents as a woman licensed and ordained to preach the gospel of Jesus Christ and be the full-time publisher at Black Authors Rock, God's Word remains true.

The impact of touching lives globally by my faith walk has changed the lives of many internationally. People care about titles, but only what you do for Christ truly matters. It's humbling to know how people see His light through me and desire to follow in His direction. Sometimes, I was the only God that some people experienced. It's an honor.

The GPS that brought me from Minnesota to Mississippi in 2010 was the foundation to this very chapter in my life. I had to live my faith out loud, as sometimes I was the only example of God that some see. Saying "YES" to God ultimately affects your outcome in life. Faith is the substance of things hoped for and the evidence of things not seen. I did not know eleven years ago that I would have this confidence in the unknown while looking forward with expectation from the GPS (God's Perfect Situation).

Just like the GPS, God sits high and looks low; He sees things before we do, and it's all according to our belief in Him. In the unknown! We must trust Him in all things! Because faith is personal and never private.

Dr. LaTracey McDonald, a recognized professional writers' consultant, edifies, equips, and enlightens aspiring writers to become published authors. She's the chief executive officer, publisher, and founder of Black Authors Rock. She leads the Black Authors Rock online community for aspiring writers and authors and is the founder of Capstone Experience, Inc. Dr. LaTracey has a master's degree in nonprofit management and executive leadership from St. Thomas University and has an honorary doctorate of humanitarianism from Global of International Alliance. She is an ordained minister licensed to preach the Gospel of Jesus Christ, specializing in youth ministry. In addition to her ministry gifts and talents, Dr. McDonald possesses a profound skill set in desktop publishing, business development, and motivational speaking.

CHAPTER 24

When God's Path Differs from Desires, Follow Him

By Bryant Lavender

In May 2014, I gazed at the NFL draft on the television while subconsciously replaying the moments leading up to this day. During Pro-Day, I executed all drills perfectly that proved to the scouts I could play at the professional level. A week before the draft, a Miami scout contacted me with good news. He told me I was on their leader board to be drafted. Automatically, I prepared myself to receive a follow-up call. I felt in my heart that I was going to be a Miami Dolphin.

The NFL draft is a three-day event filled with high emotions and expectations. Based on my statistics and my school's caliber, my heart was set on being drafted on day three. On day two, I received a phone call from family members letting me know that they wanted to give my friend and me a draft party. Shortly after agreeing to have the party, I felt immense pressure fall on me — pressure because there was a possibility I would not get drafted, and honestly, I didn't want everyone to see the emotions that would follow if I wasn't drafted. These emotions would be fueled by the failed promise I made to my father. Eight years before this day, I leaned toward my father's casket and said, "Pops, I'm going to the NFL." I honestly didn't want people to see me at that moment immersed in my emotions if I did not get drafted; however, once I agreed to the party, it was out of my control.

Day three had arrived. My friend's name was called. Filled with excitement, I jumped and yelled for him as if it were me. The day went on, and my name still hadn't been called. With apprehension in my heart, I went to the party. The encouragement I received along this journey was the only thing that helped keep my nerves at bay. My cell phone suddenly rang, and I jumped up with nerves running through my body. When I answered it, it was not the call I was hoping for. The call I received that day was from an agent whom I had planned on signing with, but he advised me that I would not be able to sign with him, that I needed to get myself a workout. That was the reason I was trying to sign with him, so he could help me get the workout! When the call ended, I removed myself from the crowd. I could feel the pent-up emotions getting ready to explode. As I got closer to my car, tears began to cascade down my face. The failure that I wanted to hide came out. I started to question myself and wonder why God hadn't rescued me as he had done in the past. If He knows the desires of my heart, why didn't he give me the outcome I desired? I couldn't stop asking, "What made this time any different?"

Feeling rejected, I asked God, "What do I do now?" Immediately the thought of a book came to mind. In 2013, I promised God that I would write a book once I was got a break from football. I assumed this was the break God was waiting for. I didn't know how to go about publishing a book, nor did I want to at first. I was still hurt by football. However, I made the promise to God, which I wanted to honor. I made a phone call to the author who had said she would help me. What made this difficult was the idea of sharing my innermost thoughts with the world. I didn't want to be rejected again. I wanted to prove that I was more than just a kid with shoulder pads, cleats, and a jersey. I went into a recovery phase because I knew the journey ahead would require all I had. I pulled out all my journals I'd kept over the years. Re-reading my journal entries, it hit me: I had to step off the boat as Peter did to walk on water. I had to trust God completely.

As the release date approached, my nerves slowly took over. I was opening up a completely different side to the world. Nobody knew what I wrote. Was I ready to showcase this talent to the world? I stepped out on faith and the promise I had made. This assignment stretched, pulled, and eventually pushed me out of my comfort zone. My thoughts and experiences were out in the world. Some people purchased the book because they knew me, while others purchased the book because it was appealing to them. Days after the release, notification pings started coming in. This was the confirmation I needed to let me know I was able to reach someone.

As I scrolled through the comments, my self-doubt slowly left me. One comment read, "Lav, do you have any more books? I have got to get one. I started reading my friend's copy of your book just to see what you were talking about, and it spoke to me. I want my copy."

It was God's way of saying, "I'm not finished with you." Through my obedience, Christ has given me the ability to speak life to people. I've used this gift to motivate individuals on the purpose God has bestowed on their lives. It is important to know that everyone will not understand your aspirations; however, know that God will place you where you need to be the moment you start living for Him.

Since 2014, I have released four books and am working on the fifth one, "Encounters," about relationships that either grow or die.

My friend, I know there is something that has risen to the forefront of your mind as you read this chapter. Fear of rejection is attempting to grip and cripple you. This feeling has numbed you to the point where you feel that you are not worthy to do that thing God has spoken to you to do. I want to tell you: Peter didn't know what he was getting himself into when he asked Jesus to tell him to come to meet him on the water. With hesitation, Peter stepped off the boat, and in amazement, was walking on water. He was able to only because he trusted Jesus. During your journey, you must step

COMPLETELY off the boat and trust the vision He has put within you. As you gain or regain your fire for your purpose in life, watch how God works miracles in you and through you.

Bryant Lavender is a native of Gulfport, Miss. He has bachelor's degree from the University of South Alabama. He published his first book in 2014 and since then has published three more books and is working on his fifth. As a speaker and author, he lives to be a spark plug to push people into their purpose.

CHAPTER 25

Worthy

By Sherry Moxley Seaman

I was attending an all-team appreciation night at Northwood Church when I was called to the stage to accept an award for my leadership role in the new launch of our fourth campus. Pastor Stephen DeFazio said he wanted to recognize several people who had been serving and giving tirelessly and who were impacting people in ways that only God could do through them. When my name was called, I was so moved and shocked I began to cry. I proudly and humbly walked to the stage to receive this great honor. I am in such awe of what God has not only done in my life, but through me; how He has and is equipping me to help build His kingdom. So, let me show you what God has done for me, to me, and through me.

For many years, I carried guilt and shame about all the messes I had made in my life. I never felt like I could have a place in my old life or in my home church. I felt like people were judging me and wondering how I could ever really worship God. I allowed the devil to hold me in bondage for years. But then, through many small groups at Northwood, much prayer, and counsel from my dear friend and business partner (whom I met at a small group), I began to shed the old and live out the new. Have you ever felt like you were unworthy to worship Jesus or talk about Him? For many years I had been running from my past; that was me.

When I began to attend Northwood, I was asked to be on the host team, and I immediately said yes. I love to talk, greet, and meet people, love to love on people and make them feel welcome. I can do that. I did it well. I then was asked to join a small group, so I did. In that small group, I began to see many women just like me. They had a past. Then, months later, I was asked to serve as a captain on the host team, and I hesitantly said, "Are you sure you want me?"

They said, "Yes," so I did it. Why did I hesitate? Well, it wasn't because I knew I couldn't lead people; it was because I wondered how I would pray with people out loud. Being a leader in a church is so different from being a leader in business — or is it? The next small group I joined was our Freedom Group. Wow! Oh, wow! This was where I was able to let it all go! Not only did God use that group to heal me, this experience helped me to begin shedding the past and to see myself the way He does. He also used this group to connect me with Dorothy Wilson, with whom I am now in business and whom I hold dear as a friend, prayer warrior, and a true sister in every sense of the word.

My husband and I then were asked to go on a mission trip to Guatemala, and this was life-changing. This was work every day in a country where so many people needed healing and to be set free of oppression and addiction, where they needed to be set free of guilt and shame. I worshiped with folks who didn't understand my language, nor did I understand them, but we all had one thing in common, and that was Jesus. We all served the same amazing God. I can remember praying over people, watching them be healed and set free. I, myself, received a healing on a mountain in one of the villages we were in. I saw the Holy Spirit move in a way I had never seen before in my life. After returning from this trip, I knew it was time to begin small groups again, and while thinking of which group I wanted to attend, I was asked to co-lead. I am truly just in awe of what others were seeing in me that I still couldn't really see in myself. This was not just any group but Freedom Group, where others can be set free. I used my testimony and my walk with God to pour into others and help them receive the same healing. You just want people to be changed the way you were changed and feel the presence of God and the love of God and the feeling of no guilt, no shame!

Shortly after this, our church announced it was going to open a fourth location. My husband said we should help. I agreed. I thought we would continue to be on the host team, welcoming people and greeting people. Little did I know that the pastors had other plans for me. They asked if I would not olny be on the launch team, but also be the kids' ministry coordinator. They asked if I would be a kids' ministry coordinator. I thought, "I love kids, but that is too big of a responsibility, and there is no way you want me to do that."

See, the closer you get to God, the more the devil shows up. After all that I have already experienced in my new journey in Christ, he was still after me. I said I would think about it, but I knew I was not going to accept. Two days later, I was driving to one of our church leadership meetings, and my dear friend Nancy Brindley from Atlanta, Ga., who introduced me to my husband and to Northwood, called and said, "Hey, I do not know what this means, but I am supposed to tell you something." She said the Lord told her I was supposed to be involved in a kids' ministry; I was blown away, first, because I had not shared anything with her yet; two, because I was prepared to walk in that meeting and politely decline the request to be the kids' coordinator of that campus.

I wanted to just go to church and serve once a month; that was what I was used to. I quickly said to Nancy, "Oh my goodness. Are you sure the Lord told you this?"

She said, "Yes."

I went into the meeting and told Pastor Tom I would accept the role. He said, "You have leadership skills; you can do this." I knew I had leadership skills, but not this kind. I had led women in other businesses for years, but what he did not know was that I felt so inadequate, so unworthy for this ministry, to serve and to lead women in a ministry that I believe is one of the single most important ministries of a church: our kids! But what I have found is that God equips me every day. He has planted in my heart a desire like I have never had before. What I quickly realized is that God and others see me so differently from how I see myself. They see my present and my future, and Jesus all over my life, not my past.

We get stuck in our past, and then we miss the blessing. If I had declined, just look at what I would have missed out on. This is all God, not me, but I get to be blessed along the way.

I recently lost my mother, and my world has been turned upside down. To lose your mother, your best friend, your rock, causes such pain that is so deep, so real, and so painful, that if I did not have Jesus as my anchor, my true comforter, I could be in a different place right now. Yes, the hole in my heart is real, but one of the many things I am so thankful for is a recent visit during Thanksgiving. When my mother was here, she visited our new fourth campus and saw the work we were doing to launch this church. She was so impressed, she said to me, "I am so proud of you!" Did I really believe her? There is a part of me that still wonders whether my parents were proud of me. I am forever changed and grateful that neither she nor my heavenly Father ever gave up on me and prayed me through.

Recently, my mother's best friend of 50 years, Naomi Cheeks, called to check on me, and in that hour-long conversation, she said to me, "Sherry, I just talked to your mother before she got sick and went in the hospital, and she said, 'Naomi, I am ready to go to heaven.' Let's go." She knew her work was done here on earth. Naomi then added, "Your mother told me in that recent conversation how proud she was of you."

I began to weep. I said, "Thank you, Naomi. I am so grateful."

Thinking about that night when I walked to the stage to receive that award, I never would have believed that I would be living my faith out loud the way I am now. I am helping my church impact a city. This is so amazing.

My mother was a person of strong faith, and she showed her faith in how she loved others every day. I am blessed to have an opportunity to walk in her footsteps, touching the lives of others.

I can't image my life without Jesus, and I want everyone to experience what I have in Him.

Sherry Moxley Seaman is intentional about living with priorities of faith first, family second, and career third. She was raised in the ministry for 54 years, but never felt worthy to serve the ministry until five years ago. Her most current role in the fourth campus launch of her church is kids' coordinator and small group leader. She is a partner is multiple media companies.

CHAPTER 26

Pushing Past 'What If"

By Kathy P. Rogers

The night I left my mother at a nursing home was one of the hardest of my life. The emotions I experienced the next day when I went back, and she looked at me in surprise and said, "I thought you weren't coming back," were almost crippling.

My mother spent 30 days in that nursing home. During my daily visits I began to observe the residents of the facility. As I did, I saw that my mother was not the only person there who struggled with feelings of loneliness, depression, and isolation. As I looked at these people, I remembered the regular visits and summers spent with my grandparents and the experiences of growing up with my Great Uncle Mitt living in our home. I saw the faces of my elderly family members, and God began to break my heart for them.

This experience was the impetus for what has become Adopt A Grandparent Day, a one-day event where volunteers visit with residents of local nursing homes in the lower six counties of South Mississippi.

Before I go further, let me go back to the beginning of the story. My father passed away in 2008, and my mother continued to live alone in her home until 2011. I vividly remember my Aunt Juanita's call and her words: "I called your mother, and she answered the phone, but she can't speak." I immediately left work for her home; when I arrived, she met me at the back door with a look of despair. She appeared fine physically, but could not speak; she had suffered a stroke. During her hospital stay, she struggled to speak but could sing clearly; she began to sing the old hymn "I'll Fly Away" over and over. The unknown of her condition and the words of the hymn made for an emotional time for us all. When she was discharged, she came to live with my husband and me, permanently.

As I look back over my life, I can see God's hand in the Biblical foundation laid down for me regarding His admonition to care for the elderly. It shaped my view of family and my belief that, as much as is within my power, it is my responsibility to see that they are cared for.

Personally, and as a business owner, I look for ways to give back to my community that align with my values and demonstrate my faith. I'm sure you do the same. As we mapped out our plans for 2014, we wondered if perhaps, what if, we could make a difference by encouraging volunteers to visit nursing homes.

I believe "what if" can cripple or encourage you. Why is it that "what if" brings to mind the worst possible scenario instead of the best possible outcome? Why not choose to believe that God is for you and not against you or that He has good plans for your life? I choose to embrace "what if," believing the outcome will be for my good. I am a person with what has been lovingly and not-so-lovingly called "bulldog tenacity." Until I am proven wrong, I believe I can accomplish what I set out to do. I refuse to allow myself to be crippled by a fear driven "what if." I believe fear is part of the plan of the enemy to steal, kill, and destroy the vision and passion God wants to give us, and that it tends to attract to us the very thing we fear. We often receive what we expect; we expect to be defeated or rejected, so we believe we are so even if it is not true. Take the time to read the first few chapters of the story of Job. He says in Job 3:25: "For the thing that I greatly feared has come upon me, and what I dreaded has happened to me."

With this believing mindset, help from our staff, and encouragement from others, my husband, Lee, and I began our journey to bring our "what if" into reality. I reached out to local newspaper and media companies to help us promote our event, and they embraced our vision. For our first event in 2014 we visited 19 facilities in three counties with about 225 volunteers. Success!

Each year we worked hard to expand our impact. We reached out to other local businesses for their support to help with finances and volunteers. We became a 501c3 non-profit organization in 2015. In 2016, we expanded our reach to six counties. We now serve 35 facilities and are looking for more to add each year. The lives of the nursing home residents and the lives of our volunteers are being changed.

Through our efforts, many more people have become aware of the plight of the residents of nursing homes and the fact that Pre-Covid, 60 percent of residents had no outside visitors. With the restrictions necessitated by Covid, their everyday feelings of loneliness and isolation are even greater.

Knowing these feelings were even greater for residents this, year we began to look for different ways to fulfill our mission. Instead of bringing volunteers into the nursing homes, our volunteers helped us create treasure boxes full of items to give to the residents. Volunteers decorated the boxes, colored and laminated pictures, made cards and letters, and donated an assortment of items to be included in the boxes, which were then dropped off at the facilities by more volunteers. The gratitude and enthusiasm from the employees of each facility proved to us that we make a difference, not only to the residents but also to the staff! Because we were willing to look outside the box of how we normally do things, we made a difference in spite of the challenges of 2020.

Because of the heartbreak I experienced, Adopt A Grandparent Day was founded. Because of the awareness we have generated, people are on their own reaching out to nursing home residents, elderly family, and neighbors. They are choosing to make a difference. Individuals, churches, businesses, and families are being the hands and feet of Christ as they bring life to the vision God gave us to recognize, honor, and value the lives of the elderly in our society, to provide them with love and affection with no strings attached.

What about you? Are you making a difference for His glory? I encourage you to reevaluate your vision for your life. Is it simply good or a God-given vision? He has given gifts to each of us to use for His glory; are you using yours? I encourage you to believe again that you were born for such a time as this, that the gifts He has given you and what the Holy Spirit has deposited inside of you can be used to make a difference in the lives of others.

Kathy Rogers is vice president of Marston Rogers Group, a financial services and life insurance business. She is a life planner and a business coach. Her passion is to help individuals and businesses evaluate their current situation with an eye toward their future. Her 40 years' experience as a business owner combined with her life experiences as a parent and caregiver for elderly parents uniquely equip her to understand the challenges people face. She is the co-author of four books, founder and executive director of Adopt A Grandparent Day, and serves on the board of the Women's Resource Center.

CHAPTER 27

Praying into my Purpose

By Angela Houston

Before I decided to step out on the water, fear was my greatest companion. I was afraid I would be wrong, misunderstood, and rejected. You see, that is what appeared to be my lot in this life. I was a divorced widow with three children and dated a person, "the devil," for three years. We'd recently broken up. My children struggled with the loss of their father because they were Daddy's girls. I stayed at the feet of Jesus for months looking for answers and healing; God gave me Isaiah 54. I would read this chapter daily.

The two verses that tended to inspire me the most were Isaiah 54:2: "Enlarge the place of thy tent and let them stretch forth the curtains of thine habitations: spare not, lengthen thy cords, and strengthen thy stakes." And Isaiah 54:17: "No weapon that is formed against thee shall prosper, and every tongue that shall rise against thee in judgment thou shalt condemn."

My pastor at that time kept telling me that I was a prayer warrior and a prophet. He said he saw me praying for people in groups. He would encourage me and push me. At work, I was praying with women and leading them to Christ. That was my first step. I used a Red Prayer Book as a ministering tool at work. When I decided to start my first prayer meeting, I was so nervous, but I decided I needed walk in my calling. I was tired of walking in fear and doubt. During this time, I was confessing 2 Timothy 1:7: "For God hath not given us the spirit of fear; but of power, and of love, and of a sound mind."

My obstacles seemed to be many; however, 90 percent of them were battles in my mind. I realized that I had to start where I was. I had allowed my circumstances and my surroundings to dictate my steps. God was not directing me, fear was. What tools did I have? A space in my home for prayer and the Holy Spirit.

I overcame my fears in prayer. By doing this, I gained more confidence in what God could do through me and stopped relying on my own strengths. I began praying the Word of God, and the Word became alive in my life. When the prayer meeting began, I just said, "Holy Spirit, you take over every aspect of what will happen here tonight." And boy, did He! He showed me what to say, what to pray, where I needed to stand, and why I was standing there. IT WAS AWESOME. God not only delivered the ladies in the group, but ME AS WELL. My eyes were opened on a level that I could not have imagined. That gave me the charge that God had been trying to show me for decades.

This was the beginning of my prayer line. I meet with women at least once a month for prayer and encouragement. I am part of a prayer group called Pray, Women, Pray, and we pray for women all over the world. It is a JOY to pray and see how God is changing people's lives. I have seen marriages restored, children saved and people set free.

I can remember praying with a couple, and I saw their married child arguing about a car decision. The mother called the daughter and confirmed what God had spoken. This encouraged and gave wisdom to that young couple.

For someone who is struggling like I was, I say that you have nothing to lose but everything to gain. There is no greater feeling than seeing someone's life change before your eyes. Step out on faith.

Before turning my life over to Christ Jesus, I was just a lost, wandering soul without any direction or purpose, just letting life happen to me without any plans. I was leaning on my own understanding.

Now Christ orders my steps. I seek Him first in all that I do, and I let him direct my path.

Angela Houston is a native of Augusta, Ga. She is a mother and grandmother. She is currently employed with the state government as a policy interpreter. She holds a degree in sociology and holds certification as a life coach. She is the founder of Mourning Into Dancing Ministries. As an author, mentor, speaker, and prophetess, she uses her gifts to edify the body of Christ and draw the lost to salvation.

CHAPTER 28

The Power of Positivity

By Latisha "Positivity Tish" Price

When I decided to leave my dream job after 17 years, it felt like the mother eagle was pushing me out of the nest. I loved my job and loved the people I worked with, until I began to have "that feeling" — you know that feeling when something within you is off. It was a feeling of wanting to burst out of my own skin. That's when I knew God was moving me out of my comfort zone.

You see, I felt safe, secure, and committed to my job and the people around me, but the time had come when I had to release my job and take charge of my future. I have worked since I was 16 years old, and that's all I've ever known. Life was very comfortable and safe.

My faith walk forward began on June 1, 2018, my last day working a full-time job and my first day of freedom. I'm talking about mental and spiritual freedom. I didn't realize how much I was caged in by the norm in my culture: go to school, college, work, and retire/die. That was pretty much "the life." I wanted something more; I wanted to leave a legacy, and I wanted to make an impact on this earth.

Once the decision was made to create my exit — and this was two years before I actually did it — I began to listen to thought leaders, read the book, "The Secret," and listen to positive motivational speakers to keep my mind on the plan to leave. To me the move was not easy, because when I shared it with the people who are close to me, they asked, "Why would you leave a job with benefits?" I was also told I was crazy to leave a job with nothing else to go to. That's when I realized God gave this to me and not to them. I had to stay focused and wear blinders, because this is what I had to do.

Galatians 6:9 states, "Let us not become weary in doing good, for at the proper time we will reap a harvest if we do not give up."

Once I got that taste of freedom, I decided to make some major changes in my life, such as working and serving in church, spending more time with my family, and working my business like never before. I surround myself with people who love to win and teach you how to win.

Then something unexpected began to happen. I had decided to use a social media platform to post inspirational quotes and nuggets to help people start their day on a positive note. My good friend Brittany always called me "Positivity Tish." Little did she know I struggled through the negativity daily. People began to tell me how much I inspired them and to keep posting because they were seeing the right quote at the right time.

Of course, most don't realize that when I post, I'm not only encouraging others, I'm also cheering myself on. You can teach others only what you've learned or are learning yourself.

The more I posted and the more courageous I became as an entrepreneur, the more I could see that I was making an impact on others. I love the feeling I get when people privately message me and say, "You have made my day; thank you." I know I'm serving people and my purpose.

I guess I just didn't realize the power of what I was doing, but there is so much negativity in the world that even small drops of positivity can have a powerful punch.

One of my favorite quotes is, "Don't give other people permission to ruin your day." Many people allow this to happen, but I want you to know that you have a choice about how you will live and feel each day.

You can choose to align yourself with God's promises and what His word says about you, or you can choose to believe the negativity spewing forth from others. Remember, hurt people hurt other people. You can choose not to pick up their weight.

After reading this chapter, make a declaration right now: I no longer give other people permission to _____. Did you know being embarrassed is an emotion? You are giving people permission to activate that emotion.

Each day, I choose to greet others with, "Great morning!" It's my declaration. It's my choice to have a great day. I have chosen life and life more abundantly.

Proverbs 18:21 puts it this way: "The tongue has the power of life and death." Your words can either speak life, or your words can speak death. Our tongues can build others up, or they can tear them down.

Latisha Lewis Price is a Mary Kay sales director based in Gulfport, Miss. She holds a bachelor's degree in business administration and is a graduate of The University of Southern Mississippi. She is the office manager for Gulf Coast Woman Magazine and worked for the Sun Herald newspaper in the advertising/marketing department for seventeen years. She also worked in the corporate office of the YMCA, as a cake decorator at a local grocery store, and worked in the business office at South Mississippi Regional Center (SMRC). Working at SMRC she learned to have compassion for people with disabilities. She is married to Danny Price and has a bonus son, Danterrio Johnson.

CHAPTER 29

How Can You Ask Me for a Drink?

By Jessica Rankin

When a Samaritan woman came to draw water, Jesus said to her,
"Will you give me a drink?" ...The Samaritan woman said to him, "You are a Jew, and I am a
Samaritan woman. How can you ask me for a drink?"
John 4:7-9

As I served in the nursery at church and listened to the testimonies of the women serving alongside me, I knew Jesus was asking me a question just as He had done to the Samaritan woman at the well. "Will you take your place in the body of Christ?" I knew Jesus was leading me to find my place among my brothers and sisters in the family of Christ, but just like the Samaritan woman, I found myself asking, "How can you ask this of me?" I can imagine the scene at the well, the Samaritan woman looking around for whom Jesus was talking to. When she realized He was looking at her, she pointed to herself and asked Jesus, "Are you sure you're talking to me?, I am not worthy of that request. Surely, you aren't asking me. Are you? You know I am a Samaritan woman, right? And you're a Jew. There are countless reasons why you shouldn't ask this of me. Are you sure?"

In 2013, my husband and I began regularly attending church services. I sat in the sanctuary each Sunday with a hurt on my heart I thought would never be healed. You see, in 2010 my husband and I lost our first son. He was stillborn at 32 weeks gestation. Since then, I had been struggling with a guilt so profound it had paralyzed me from living a full life. My son had died due to an undiagnosed blood clotting disorder, but to me, I was to blame. I felt that I was his mother, and as such, should have protected him. I should have known there was a problem. This guilt led to shame, which led to isolation, which led to self-doubt, which led to my deciding I would never be good enough.

As we continued to attend church, I sat each week jealous of the believers surrounding me. They seemed so sure of their chosen status. They worshiped with such freedom, hands lifted to the one they knew defined them. But I remained sure that this freedom was beyond my reach.

We continued attending church, and in August of that year, I began to serve in the church nursery. I began to learn about who God is, about His promises to us, about His love for us, and about who He says I am in His kingdom. The women I served alongside shared their testimony about how

God had spoken to them and changed their lives. I began to feel God was asking me a question, asking me to be a part of the body of Christ. A believer. I began to glimpse hope; I began to wonder if God did have something for me.

This hopeful glimpse caused me to ask the same types of questions the Samaritan women had asked Jesus: "Are you talking to me? Surely, you aren't asking me, are you? I am not worthy of that request. You know I am just me, right? I am not like your other daughters. I have failed. My son is dead because I couldn't protect him. I am scared every day that I will fail again. I am terrified every day that something will happen to the family I have left. I lay awake at night sometimes and wonder if I will live until tomorrow. I live a life dominated by selfish ambition so that others won't see me the way that I see me -- a failure, and Jesus, to be honest with you, I even doubt if you are the Messiah. I doubt it all! Are you sure you want me, Jesus? Are you sure, because honestly it seems like there are better options?"

After the Samaritan woman had essentially told Jesus, "It seems like there are better options out there... just saying," Jesus answered her in John 4:10 by saying, "If you knew the gift of God and who it is that asks you for a drink, you would have asked Him, and He would have given you living water." With these words he piqued her curiosity. I imagine she thought, "living water? How do I get some of that?"

For the next several chapters she sits with Jesus and listens to Him as He explains that He knows exactly whom He is asking. He knows all about her past and who she really is. He asked her for water knowing all the reasons that she thought would make her unworthy. Jesus took a woman who had been questioning her worth, and He laid a hope in front of her so profound that her chains of self-doubt couldn't keep her down. She said yes to His question and essentially yes to Him and took His message to her people, spreading the gospel to others. She took her place in the body of Christ.

When I felt Jesus asking me, I gave Him all the reasons He shouldn't choose me. I just knew the damage was too great, but the hopeful glimpses I was experiencing pulled me to the feet of Jesus to listen. While I sat at His feet, an amazing thing happened. He explained how He knew exactly whom He was asking. He knew all about my past and who I really am. He knew my struggles with guilt, shame, doubt, and selfish ambition. Knowing all this, He chose me anyway. After He told me He chose me, He began to heal my heart of all those things I thought made me unworthy.

He led me to forgive myself, to let the guilt of losing our son fall away. He led me to realize I wasn't to blame for my undiagnosed medical condition. He told me to not be ruled by a spirit of fear. He told me He had made a place for me, so there was no need for selfish ambition. He told me to live a life free of those guilts and fears that had been holding me down. He told me to live a life covered in His cleansing blood, the cleansing blood He died for me to have. He told me while I am covered with Him, the Father will see me. Just me. His chosen daughter walking in purpose. A daughter operating daily, so that she, like her sister the Samaritan woman, can bring the gospel to others and spread the good news of Jesus Christ.

This year makes my eighth year serving in the nursery at church. I am now serving in a leadership capacity and leading other women to say yes to the call of Jesus. In 2021, I am releasing a book sharing my testimony about healing after losing our son. I pray God will use this book to show other women they are worthy of the healing power of Christ.

For all of you who feel you have lists of things that make you unworthy, bring them to the feet of Jesus. Tell Him why you are not worthy, and He will tell you He chose you already. Our sister the Samaritan women went on to share her testimony and led many others to Christ. You can do this, too. You, too, have a place in the kingdom of God, a place where you can live your faith out loud. A place that God has already prepared for you. Now go and find it, my friend.

Jessica Rankin, 38, of Gulfport, Miss., is a wife, home-school mom of two boys, author, speaker, consultant, and entrepreneur. She is the owner of The Safe Food Culture, LLC, a regulatory and training consulting firm.

CHAPTER 30

Courage to Choose Life

By Tiffany D. Bell

As a little girl, I never had any real dreams or aspirations to become anything specific. Most little girls grow up dreaming of marrying someone tall and handsome like their father. Not me. I only knew that I wanted to dress up with heels, makeup, and a briefcase each day.

When it was time to begin to plan for college, the only thing that I could see myself doing was teaching, something that I have seen modeled since kindergarten. I knew that I did not want to join the military, so becoming a teacher seemed doable. It was an easy choice, but I had no passion for teaching students.

As it turns out, I ended up going in a completely different direction. Amazingly enough, I did, indeed, join the military! And I loved it! It was wonderful to travel, meet new people, try new foods, learn new skills, all while serving my country. It was a great adventure until I received a pregnancy diagnosis. My world came tumbling down. I was only 19 years old. Never in a million years did I expect to be "that girl." I was always considered to be a good girl to my family and friends. Things like this didn't happen to quiet girls like me.

As I sat on the exam table, thoughts rushing to and fro, I fought to gather my breath. How was this going to affect my career? Would my family disown me? How was I going to take care of a child?

I was nearly 1,300 miles away from my family. They would never look at me the same. How would I live past the guilt and shame of getting pregnant out of wedlock? My future looked less than bleak. I had to figure a way out. Abortion — that's the answer, I thought. I could abort the baby. No one would ever know. Well, no one aside from the father. I had to tell him.

It turns out that he was in complete agreement with terminating the pregnancy. But I would have to go at it alone. He wasn't able to contribute financially. I, too, had other financial obligations. There was no way that I could pay for something like that. How would I even begin to plan? Where would I go to have an abortion performed? Would anyone find out? How do I keep this a secret? So many questions, and I had no answers and no one to discuss my situation with. All I know is that I needed a way out — quickly. The sheer weight of the stress paralyzed me from taking any of the necessary steps to seek help.

One day turned into a week. A week turned into a month. One month turned into two. Before I knew it, I was four months pregnant. It was too late in my mind to have the abortion. I had begun to show a little.

I also still needed to let my family know. I was so afraid, so I procrastinated for a few more weeks. I now was 21 weeks pregnant. I had to let them know. Little did I know that I would go into preterm labor just a few short weeks later. My son would be born nearly 16 weeks early. He was 2 lbs. 9 oz. and beautiful! It was love at first sight.

I had always prided myself in being a responsible person. I didn't make all the right decisions, no one is perfect, but I knew for sure that every decision that I made from this day forward counted more than ever. My life no longer belonged to just me. I had another little person that was tied to every decision. There were certain things that I could no longer do — and places that I could no longer go, and people that I needed to disconnect with.

During this time, I began to seek a real relationship with God. I had always believed in God, but I can't say that I had a sincere relationship. I would pray from time to time when things got tough. I went to church, too, but honestly, I didn't understand how the cross applied to my life. I did okay for a while.

It's been 26 years since my pregnancy. My life and lifestyle have changed dramatically since then. Today, I am well aware of how Christ's death, burial, and resurrection affect my life. I understand how much God loved us by giving us His son. The fantastic part of the story is that God didn't sacrifice Himself. He gave up His son. As a parent, I would gladly give up my life for my children, but would I give my sons up for someone else's life? That's love. It's incredible when you think of it.

I now understand a woman when she finds herself in an unplanned pregnancy. I know what it feels like to be alone hundreds of miles away with little to no help or support. I can relate to the need for a quick fix. The fear, guilt, and shame are real.

The disappointment that she experiences within her mind when she attempts to share her predicament with family, friends, or the baby's father can be paralyzing.

My mother found herself in the same situation, except she was raped. In some people's opinion, she was justified in choosing abortion. She indeed considered it. She instead stopped and spoke with someone who encouraged her to make an adoption plan. Her courage was remarkable. I am the result of that rape.

Her courage to choose life for me has opened the door to me to help others to do the same. Today, I work as a director for a pregnancy care center. We encourage women to make positive life choices when faced with an unplanned pregnancy. Women need a safe environment to share their fears and uncertainties. They also need to know the love that God has for them and that He has good plans for their lives and the life of their unborn child. As I share my story, women feel accepted, understood, and empowered to choose life.

Twenty-six years ago, I decided to change my lifestyle after my son's birth. It wasn't easy, but my habits, priorities, and mindset changed. But the changes were necessary. Ultimately, those changes built a platform for me to share the gospel. I can use my story to encourage others, and I can create community partnerships for the pregnancy center. Knowing that I am building God's kingdom, making a difference in my community, and equipping women with the good news of the gospel give purpose to a terrifying season of my life as a 19-year-old. God can redeem all things and use them for His glory. I am empowered to do more.

I am using my faith to equip women to believe in God for provision, wisdom, and strength. It takes courage, but it is possible. I believe that God desires to use all our stories to grow His kingdom.

Before I began this journey, I was a quiet, timid person. I was insecure and unsure how to share my faith and my story. Over the years, I have identified my life purpose and want to help others. I connect people to resources, people to people, and people to God. Everything that I do relates to that.

I have grown in my faith and love helping others to do the same.

For anyone struggling to express their faith in a more impactful way, I would say first to pray. The Holy Spirit continually speaks. He wants to use us. His wisdom and direction are there for the taking. Then believe God. The advice that the Holy Spirit gives is reliable. You can trust that He will lead you the correct way. And finally, get up and get moving! Don't wait for others to affirm you. Don't wait for everything to be perfectly aligned. Things will begin to fall into place as you move in faith.

Make no excuses nor allow yourself to be discouraged. With the help of the Holy Spirit, you can and will make an impact on your portion of the world!

Tiffany D. Bell is a multidimensional leader, influencer, and communal advocate. As the executive director of the Women's Resource Center of Gulfport, Tiffany encourages women to make positive life choices. Tiffany is co-director of Success Women's Conference, which was recently named a Top 10 Conference for Professional Women by Essence Magazine. Tiffany holds a degree in radiological health services. She is an honorary commander for Keesler Air Force Base 2nd Air Force, 81st Medical Group. She served as a director of Keesler Air Force Protestant Women's Group and was a Bible study leader for many years. She is former co-chairman on the board of trustees for Lighthouse Business and Professional Women, a director for the Biloxi Bay Area Chamber, and treasurer for the 2019-2020 year of the Kiwanis Club of Orange Grove, of which she was recently nominated for Lay Person of the Year award. She received the 2019 Tom Tandler Lifetime Achievement Award. Tiffany is the mother of two sons, and she is a grandmother.

CHAPTER 31

Called to a Life of Adventure

By Sheila Farr

Living for the Lord will make you do things you never believed you could do. That's the beauty of this adventure called life. Now, we all know an adventure is not really an adventure without a little risk involved, so you have to know that when you are called to serve the Lord, the road is going to be nothing less than a pathway filled with more twists and turns than the human mind could possibly imagine. The beauty of that, however, is that He truly equips each of us with a set of beautiful gifts to be used to navigate this journey of life. He even provides an instruction manual — our Holy Bible! We need only to remember to seek Him and His Word when we're in doubt or when we're facing fear.

Matthew is one of my favorite books in the Bible. It is one of the first that, as a new Christian, I dove into, commentary in hand and searching for its truth. Reading God's word like that made the Bible become more than just a storybook for me; it brought God's word to life right in front of my very eyes. There are so many great lessons in the Book of Matthew, but there was something about the verses that warn against burying our talents that really resonated with me. It struck me to the core, because I had spent much of my life playing small and not living like I meant it. I'd been playing things safe, walking just to the edge of my Christianity, and not really fully committing anything to anyone. I tried really hard to walk softly, share my faith politely, and not be too aggressive or bold with the way I lived or the way I shared my faith. I will tell you this, though: Once I opened my heart to the miracle-making ways of the Lord, my life was changed forever!

While we as humans sit back and wait for the Lord to deliver the news of our gifts and talents — like a big ol' Christmas gift, wrapped in all the fancy trappings — we waste our lives waiting and watching others live richly and fully. We sit back and judge, pulling inward to ourselves, and downward in our chairs, arms folded, and cut off from the world… and oftentimes cut off from the grace of God. We search; we seek; we ask for "signs," and even if our gifts are confirmed time and time again — we simply fail to see it. In this age of wanting things here and now, we often expect words from God to come to us instantaneously. We want to know our gifts, and we want them fully grown, developed, and operating at full capacity so we can just sit back and reap those blessings. The funny thing is that when we approach our relationship with the Lord in this manner, we miss out on so many things. We miss out on the opportunity to soak in the beauty of His word, and we miss out on taking the time that's needed to adequately cultivate our gifts. You don't eat the fruit the first day you plant the seed, and you definitely can't fully develop your spiritual gifts without putting them to work and using them. You've got to put in the work, using your gifts in small spaces and developing them into full-blown and full-grown gifts that are used boldly to proclaim God's love and graciousness in our lives.

Now, rest assured, the enemy will do all that he can do to distract you with negative narrative of "not good enough." He will nag at you with disappointments and failure. He will discourage you from using any sort of gift, binding your tongue, confusing your mind, and fatiguing your body to the point that you start to drift from the Lord and into those far-away places that can lead to depression, seclusion, and complacency. The good news is that we know God's word, God's love, and God's call on our life are greater than anything the enemy can throw at us, and thus we are most triumphant in life when we place our failures and disappointments in the Lord's hands and ask Him to redeem us and make all these things part of our testimony and part of the development of our spiritual gifts. We strive so hard for completion and perfection in things, but in reality, it is our imperfections and the fact that we are incomplete that make us most relatable to others. It also provides places for God to work in our lives, because He is able to show His strength when we are at our weakest! When we travel through the rough patches in life, through the hard things and the ugly places — this is only part of the cultivation of our gifts and our message to others. We can use these things to help others navigate the waters of life by sharing what we've learned through our experiences and our battles with weak faith. The world will lead us to believe we aren't worthy of being a witness, but God's word tells us otherwise, so, my friend, let me encourage you not to believe the lies of the enemy! You are loved, gifted, and treasured — and you DO have a purpose and a mission!

Most of my life I was playing small because I was waiting for some incredible announcement from God about my gifts and talents. I was insecure about so many things in my life, and because of that I suffered from shaky faith and failure after failure. I was watching everyone else live full and exciting lives of service to God, and I wanted to do the same thing. I knew I was called to serve, but because I was focused on the world and not God, my talents were slow to grow and develop. Then one day, I just started small. I began openly proclaiming the everyday miracles I saw in my life. At first, I only journaled them, but one day, God whispered for me to share it on a larger scale … and I made a Facebook post about my thankfulness and the way God works in my life. This was huge for me because it was the first time I'd been vulnerable and open about my faith and trust in God. Some people didn't like my daily thankful posts, but others came to watch for them every day. I simply stated things I saw as miracles each day: the gift of life, the richness of color in a red camellia, the smell of freshly mown grass on a warm spring afternoon – all simple things, but miraculous at the same time. Before I realized it, my open profession of thankfulness had changed my entire perspective about life and the way I approached it. It was now exciting. It was an adventure! I was sincerely full of the joy of the Lord every day just seeking out the simple miracles of each and every day, then sharing them with my friends. My posts grew into a blog, and into a book, and into speaking engagements around the globe … and I honestly felt like I was making a heavenly impact!

God's word is the truth, and His truth says that you are holy and a dearly loved child of the Heavenly Father, who is gifted and purposed to go out and make disciples of others. His word says you are to use your God-inspired gifts to share His good news, show His love, and tell everyone about His kindness, grace, and mercy. You are treasured! You are special! You are beautiful! You are gifted! You are loved! Don't bury your gifts and talents! No matter what you've done in the past or what might have been done to you, the words that God speaks about His children are real and true, so we must be certain that we make God's words become the words of our story and our purpose. We must not hide in shame, fear, or regret, but instead, we must seek out into the world – into life – as though it were an adventure, and every day we must share, share, share! Though we are but ordinary humans, we become extraordinary vessels of service through God's love and His promises! Never forget that, and even today — start to live your life like you mean it. Live as though you are truly a Kingdom heir and let your heart be filled with joy and thanksgiving. Use those talents you have! LIVE your life! God is calling each of us to a life of adventure! He has already equipped you to do the things you are called to do. There are people in the world who are waiting for you and for the gifts you have to share, no matter how large or how small. Set out on your adventure in Christ today!

"Oh, taste and see that the LORD is good; blessed is the one who takes refuge in him."
Psalm 34:8

Sheila Farr is a four-time best-selling author, business strategist, and teacher with a reputation for serving others with pure enthusiasm. She is the CEO of Biloxi, Miss.-based Gulf Coast Training & Education Services, LLC, which services multi-generational entrepreneurs and small business owners. She holds master's degrees in health and wellness counseling and adult education. Sheila is a SHRM-SCP-certified human resources director, RYT-200 yoga instructor, certified Tai Chi instructor, and was a Lean/Six Sigma black belt.

CHAPTER 32

A Graceful Break

By Jacqueline Thompson

Something is not right, I cried out! How did I lose another corporate trainer position that I had prayed for? I was specific in how I asked God to answer my prayer this time, because I didn't feel like my faith was strong enough to discern His voice. I needed an answer by a certain date, because there were three offers on the table, and guess what? It came on that exact date. The offer was extended to me on Good Friday, so I knew it was an answered prayer, and I knew it was God saying yes to the job He wanted me to have. At least that's what I thought, but obviously, I wasn't getting the message God was trying to get to me, because, if I were to press rewind-life one year, my life was turning in the right direction after a bitter, unfriendly, and heartbreaking divorce.

I was finally leaving the state of Texas to move to Atlanta to be closer to my sons after losing custody and being separated from them for a long time. I had secured a job with a major airline; I was happy, and I was blessed big to get a beautiful new home (less than a year old) from a young couple who graciously rented it to me for less than half of what it would have normally cost me to have a house like that. I started with no furniture in this home, and before I knew it, another blessing happened: it got furnished enough so that my boys now had a home to come to, and I could regain custody. Yes, life was treating me well, and I was enjoying every moment of it with a big ego (Edging God Out)!

And then it happened. Deceit caught up with me again (I've met this place too many times), and within minutes of showing up to work on a normal day, my job was snatched because I allowed someone to use a job privilege that wasn't theirs to use. God had given me everything that I prayed for, and I selfishly thought only about me! I had no job and nowhere to go except the one place I knew I could rest without judgment: my parents' home.

I couldn't fathom thinking about how I would confront that beautiful couple who was so nice to me to tell them that I could no longer live in their home. It was devastating seeing their faces drop, because I know they depended on me, based on a recommendation from a co-worker, to keep their home in perfect condition. I have witnessed God come to my rescue many times and a lot of them in the midnight hour, but for the first time, I knew what it felt like to pray about something, activate my faith, and be patient during the wait. After giving away practically everything in the house, packing up my clothes, and leaving my jeep with a mechanic where I would come back later to pick it up, a dear friend of mine paid for a bus ticket to get me to my parents' house. I knew for sure that God would rescue me again so that I didn't have to leave my boys again, but it didn't happen.

I showed up at my parents', and they knew that I did not want to be there but were there to support me until I could figure this out with God. I was angry with God, because I believed that I activated my faith wholeheartedly. I believed that He would not allow me to be separated from my sons again.

I searched for jobs. I started writing my book, "Broken," and I prayed endlessly to find a specific job that would put me back in the game of information technology as a trainer, and this time I was hired in the pharmaceutical world. I was so excited that I got to travel again. I was so excited to be where I was most passionate in my career, doing what I loved and what I am particularly good at, not to mention making a healthy salary again. So, after about three months of desperately looking for a job, I witnessed my faith being activated when the prayer I wouldn't stop praying was answered. I gladly accepted the job because I knew that it was from God, and it was back in Atlanta so, why then, after approximately seven months of doing what I have always been passionate about and right after my supervisor certified me as a trainer, was I told that I was being released because on several occasions I did not exercise good judgment? Just like that! I was so confused, hurt, and embarrassed. When I questioned HR about the why, I was told that I twice left my laptop on the bus at a corporate meeting in another state (even though both times I immediately got it back), putting the company at risk of possibly having to replace them, and how I carelessly let my corporate credit card fall through cracks and onto the ground while I was boarding a plane at the last minute with no time to have a ground employee return it, and it had to be replaced. I knew these weren't the real reasons, but I accepted their reasons and left gracefully.

About a month prior to my being released from this job, I had voiced to a peer I thought I could trust my displeasure about a racial slur made during a morning huddle. I was told that the person who made the comment was just playing and that I shouldn't take it so seriously. Afterward, the atmosphere in the office immediately changed. I also discovered that the person I confided in was awfully close to my immediate supervisor. The man who hired me and who was once very cheerful whenever we spoke and incredibly supportive of my success as a trainer was now short in conversation and distant in person. I couldn't believe it. I didn't understand it, and after I turned in my laptop, cellphone, and ID badge, I was escorted to my car. I sat in my car for what seemed like hours because the tears wouldn't stop flowing. Although I was working back in Atlanta, I technically was still living in Arkansas until I could save up enough money to permanently move back to Atlanta. That was the most emotional 506 miles I ever had to drive. I just couldn't shake the "why" off me! Does God really care for me? Does He really love me? As the tears wouldn't stop, thoughts of disobedience and disconnection from God raced through my mind. I thought, "Okay, God, so this is how you punish me? But what are you really punishing me for? What did I do wrong this time? I thought this was a breakthrough blessing, especially after I suffered from that last loss, God, so why?

It took six months of unemployment, continued prayers, a humble heart, and resilience to see beyond my circumstances before I was blessed with a not-so-prestigious job and not a very hefty salary but with a reputable company. I didn't give up on my faith, and I began to trust whatever God had in store for me. In other words, I gave him the pen to guide my future. I accepted this job with a joyful heart, a grateful heart, and I worked in excellence. Fast forward into my tenth year, my reputation is stellar. People look up to me, and I know that I will retire with this company in a prestigious leadership position.

When I look back on how I lived, I can clearly see how I never once regarded my purpose for being here, the purpose that God created just for me so that I could impact and leave an imprint of His goodness on others. I've always felt that I could do things on my own, but God continuously shows me how I'm nothing without Him. He continuously shows me that it is He who instills that drive in me to never give up, that passion to seek His wisdom and have a deeper, more intimate relationship with Him. I honestly don't believe that I ever deserved God's favor during those times when I wouldn't give Him enough of my time, but as my faith grew, I knew that He gave me grace — a graceful break!

God allowed me to experience broken moments in my life because He wanted my attention, and He wanted me to exercise my faith because I loved Him and wanted to be obedient to His word, not because I wanted faith to work for me without my obedience to Him.

I'm living my faith out loud today by keeping the focus on God and less on me. I depend on the Holy Spirit to guide me daily, because it's a gift from God, who equips His children well with all that they need. Scriptures that have built my faith are:

Trust in the Lord with all your heart, and lean not on your own understanding. In all your ways acknowledge Him and He shall direct your paths.
Proverbs 3:4-5

For we walk by faith, not by sight
2 Corinthians 5:7

But without faith it is impossible to please Him, for he who comes to God must believe that He is, and that He is a rewarder of those who diligently seek Him
Hebrews 11:6

I'm living my faith out loud by empowering others with my story — a story that that speaks to the importance of living a life of integrity vs. deceit.

When we activate our faith out of love for God, and obedience to His word, He richly rewards every area of our lives!

Jacqueline Thompson is a dual coach with a B.O.S.S. status approach. She empowers aspiring, new, and seasoned authors in seeing how life experiences and lessons translate into captivating words that come to life, and to see that when they push forward, a powerful message is born to impact others Additionally, Jacqueline helps emerging business-minded individuals uncover what's holding them back from being totally equipped in walking in their God-given purpose by encouraging them to maximize their life skills with Godly principles along their journey to destination greatness.

FROM THE PROJECT VISIONARY
Dorothy P. Wilson

Thank you for investing your time to read this book! I hope you have found yourself in at least one of these stories. As you can see, each of us have to overcome "self" to reach a point where we can begin to use our past experiences, gifts and talents to transform the lives of others. I hope you are feeling inspired to do more!

Not sure what your next step is? Why not start a weekly small group to share and discuss this book together. A Small Group Discussion Guide is available at no cost to help guide your conversations. Also, tell others about this book and encourage them to read it and start a small group, too.

As you step forward, be assured that the Holy Spirit, our helper, will be right beside you to lead the way to success!

LEAD A SMALL GROUP

DOWNLOAD SMALL GROUP DISCUSSION GUIDE

https://livingfaithoutloud.com/faithinspiration/

Made in the USA
Middletown, DE
19 April 2021